CHALLENGING THE CONSPIRACY OF SILENCE

Challenging the Conspiracy of Silence: My Life As a Canadian Gay Activist

Jim Egan

COMPILED AND EDITED BY DONALD W. MCLEOD

Toronto:

The Canadian Lesbian and Gay Archives
and
Homewood Books

CANADIAN CATALOGUING IN PUBLICATION DATA

Egan, Jim
Challenging the conspiracy of silence: my life as a Canadian
gay activist

(Canadian lesbian and gay archives; 14)
Includes bibliographical references and index.
ISBN 0-9683829-0-8

1. Egan, Jim. 2. Homosexuality — Canada. 3. Gay activists —
Canada — Biography. 4. Gay men — Canada — Biography. I.
McLeod, Donald W. (Donald Wilfred), 1957- . II. Canadian
Lesbian and Gay Archives. III. Title. IV. Series.

HQ75.8.E32A3 1998   306.76′62′092   C98-931704-8

This book has been published with the assistance of grants
from the Lesbian and Gay Community Appeal Foundation,
Toronto, and the Ontario Public Service Employees Union (OPSEU), Local 512,
Toronto.

Design, imaging, and printing by Coach House Printing,
Toronto.

Published by

The Canadian Lesbian and Gay Archives
P.O. Box 639, Station A
Toronto, Ontario M5W 1G2

(416) 777-2755
e-mail: queeries@clga.ca

Correspondence and orders to:

Homewood Books
Attn. Don McLeod
60 Homewood Avenue, Suite 502
Toronto, Ontario M4Y 2X4

Contents

This book celebrates two anniversaries:

The fiftieth anniversary of
Jim Egan and Jack Nesbit's relationship
(23 August 1998)

and

The twenty-fifth anniversary of the founding of the
Canadian Lesbian and Gay Archives
(September 1998)

Acknowledgements

This work could not have been completed without the cooperation of Jim Egan and Jack Nesbit.

I would also like to thank the following individuals for showing an interest in this project and for providing information or advice:
* David Adkin
* Harold Averill
* Rick Bébout
* Jay Cassel
* Rob Champagne
* David Churchill
* John Grube
* George Hislop
* Susan Houston
* Sidney Katz
* Gary Kinsman
* Duncan McLaren
* Philip McLeod (no relation)
* Alan V. Miller
* Chris Paulin

The collections of several libraries and archives were consulted in researching this book. I would like to thank the staff at the following institutions in particular for their kind support in finding material and answering queries:
* Archives of Ontario, Toronto
* Canadian Lesbian and Gay Archives, Toronto
* Gerber/Hart Library, Chicago
* National Library of Canada, Ottawa
* Robarts Library, University of Toronto
* Toronto Reference Library
* University of Toronto Archives

Thanks to Edna Barker for help with editing and proofreading.

Finally, I am pleased to thank the Lesbian and Gay Community Appeal Foundation, Toronto, and the Ontario Public Service Employees Union (OPSEU), Local 512, Toronto, for providing funds toward the publication of this work.

Don McLeod
Toronto
July 1998

A Note on the Illustrations

All images in this book are reproduced courtesy of Jim Egan or the Canadian Lesbian and Gay Archives, with the following exceptions:

The Savarin Hotel, Toronto, ca. 1952 (two images). Photos by William E. Whittingham, Peake and Whittingham Ltd. Reproduced with the permission of William H.G. Whittingham. From the Records of the Liquor Licence Board of Ontario, Series RG 36-8, Establishment Files, Accession 17721, Temporary Box 349, File: Savarin Hotel, Toronto. Archives of Ontario.

The Chez Paree Restaurant, Toronto, ca. 1956. Photo by Jones and Morris. Reproduced with the permission of Dan Morris. From the Records of the Liquor Licence Board of Ontario, Series RG 36-8, Establishment Files, Accession 21514, Temporary Box 30, File: Chez Paree Restaurant, Toronto. Archives of Ontario.

The Municipal Hotel, Toronto, ca. 1952 (two images). Photos by Jones and Morris. Reproduced with the permission of Dan Morris. From the Records of the Liquor Licence Board of Ontario, Series RG 36-8, Establishment Files, Accession 17721, Temporary Box 246, File: Municipal Hotel, Toronto. Archives of Ontario.

Jim and Jack as grand marshals of the Toronto Pride parade, 1995. Photo by Ali Kazimi. Reproduced with the permission of David Adkin Productions, Inc.

Back cover photo: Jack Nesbit and Jim Egan, 1995. Photo by Ali Kazimi. Reproduced with the permission of David Adkin Productions, Inc.

Preface

I am standing at the corner of Church and Wellesley streets, ground zero for Toronto's gay community. It is a beautiful, sunny day and the streets are packed with people. The date is Sunday, 29 June 1997, and the annual pride celebration — this year called Lesbian, Gay, Bisexual, Transsexual, and Transgender Pride Day — is at its height. Celebrations have been going on all week. The Metropolitan Toronto Council officially declared 23-29 June Lesbian and Gay Pride Week, and was supported by all six city or borough councils. Local bars are more crowded than usual. Business has been booming at the more than 100 neighbourhood shops and services catering mostly to lesbians and gay men. The Dyke March yesterday attracted thousands of women, and the Pride and Remembrance Run raised thousands of dollars in support of the Canadian Lesbian and Gay Archives and Toronto's AIDS Memorial.

As I navigate through the Church Street vendors' fair I can't help noticing all the familiar groups, and a few new ones, too, with their displays and flyers. Enthusiastic volunteers chat up the crowd. I arrive at the Toronto Centre for Lesbian and Gay Studies booth, where I help hand out flyers and answer questions. Waves of humanity glide by the booth. Queer people of all persuasions, in outlandish garb or buttoned-down. At least two men wear nothing at all. Straight couples, the curious. Gawkers.

By 2:30 the crowd is restless and begins to thin. Anticipation is in the air. I hurry over to the Metropolitan Toronto Reference Library where I meet my colleagues from the Canadian Lesbian and Gay Archives. We collect our signs, which read "Keeping Our Stories Alive," and are ready to march. Soon we are at the corner of Church and Bloor streets. A metallic roar announces the departure of the Dykes on Bikes, lesbian bikers who traditionally lead the parade in lieu of a police motorcycle escort. With a wave of cheers the official 1997 Pride March is under way. Michael McGaraughty, the chief marshal, barks commands through a megaphone, trying to prevent a pile up of floats, marching bands, dancers, and ordinary pedestrians right off the bat. We archivists slip in early, behind the hunk riding in the convertible vintage car sponsored by Pizza Pizza. The sun beats down as we turn the corner and head south on Yonge Street. My running shoes stick to the hot asphalt. We get spritzed by a water gun. Someone in the crowd throws glitter. People cheer. Everyone is having a great time. After a few blocks our signs grow heavy. We get light-headed from the heat and car exhaust. By the time we get to Yonge and Wellesley, the crowds have taken over most of the street, too, and squeeze the parade as through a narrow funnel. Hundreds of thousands of people — mostly gay people and their supporters — have pressed into a few blocks to celebrate gay pride. I feel overwhelmed. I ask myself, "How the hell did I end up here?" and ponder the more important question, "How did gay people in Toronto end up here?"

***

If you were a homosexual standing at the corner of Yonge and Wellesley streets in 1949, there was a good chance you wouldn't have felt comfortable with your sexual orientation. You certainly wouldn't broadcast your homosexuality. It was taboo. Back then homosexuality just wasn't talked about in polite society. It was usually viewed as a mental illness or perversion (Kinsey notwithstanding)[1]. And it was most certainly a sin. Homosexuality equalled scandal. Jobs were lost, housing was denied, lives ruined on the slightest evidence of queerness. The mere act of two consenting adult males going to bed together was then a serious criminal offence in Canada, and would remain so for the next twenty years. Police entrapment was common. Prison was a real possibility; you might be handed an indeterminate sentence if you were declared a dangerous sexual offender. Barbaric "treatments" such as electroshock therapy were not uncommon for sexual nonconformists[2].

In the Toronto of 1949 there were no clubs or support groups for gays. Those souls who did pursue their orientation sometimes hid behind a facade of marriage and conventional heterosexual respectability, only to participate in a clandestine world of quick pickups in steambaths, theatres, washrooms, or parks. Others frequented taverns or bars of mixed clientele, or did the circuit of private parties.

When one considers the reality of gay life in Toronto in 1949, the experience of Jim Egan seems fascinating. For it was in that year, and under these social and cultural circumstances, that Egan began his career as a public gay activist. The term "gay liberation" had not yet been coined. Formal "homophile" organizations did not exist in North America until the Mattachine Society was formed in Los Angeles in 1950. There were no organizations for gays in Toronto until the University of Toronto Homophile Association was founded in October 1969, just months after amendments to Canada's Criminal Code partially decriminalized homosexual acts[3].

Jim Egan is perhaps best known today for his fifty-year relationship with Jack Nesbit and for their Supreme Court challenge, in which they used the Canadian Charter of Rights and Freedoms to challenge the discriminatory exclusion of pension benefits to same-sex couples under the Old Age Security Act[4]. Jim and Jack's case received wide media coverage, and they were the grand marshals of the 1995 Pride parades in both Toronto and Vancouver. Their contribution here is extremely important, of course, but I was always more fascinated by Jim's early activism. Gay activists are common today. Today Jim and Jack might seem like sweet, harmless, grandfatherly figures, fighting for a noble cause. But in 1949 Jim's ideas and his public defence of homosexuality ran right against the grain. At that time, Jim Egan was a lone voice in the wilderness, and his actions were nothing less than revolutionary.

One oddity about Egan's activism is that it went in waves, with periods of prolific activity followed by relative quiet or a hiatus. A reconstruction of Egan's correspondence and a list of publications shows how busy he was in 1950-51, followed by a slow period until the very active years 1953-54, followed by a lull that lasted until 1959. The early 1960s saw a rise in activity, culminating in a peak during the first five months of 1964. Then everything stopped. Jim abandoned public gay activism, and he and Jack moved from Toronto to British Columbia. Jim's early career as a gay liberationist was over. His activities were eventually forgotten by most gays in the Toronto area, and were unknown to the following generation of gay liberationists active during the 1970s. Only in 1986, after more than twenty years out of the public eye, were Jim Egan and Jack Nesbit "rediscovered." Over the next decade they generated a great deal of public interest and support in their spousal benefits case, which went all the way to the Supreme Court of Canada in 1995.

The rediscovery of Jim Egan by Toronto gay activists is quite a story in itself. Sometime in 1985, a well-known Toronto librarian named Alan Suddon presented an album of clippings to retired librarian Philip McLeod. McLeod was a history buff and was fascinated by the items from the old tabloid newspapers, including examples from *Hush Free Press*, *Justice Weekly*, *True News Times (TNT)*, and others. Amongst the clippings were articles and letters by Jim Egan. McLeod wondered if Egan was still alive, and began to try to find his address. He mentioned his interest in Egan to Gerald Hannon, a journalist and member of *The Body Politic* collective. Hannon happened to look at a list of subscribers to *The Body Politic* and found Jim Egan's name and address in Courtenay, B.C. McLeod followed up, and began corresponding with Egan in 1986.

Jim Egan was flattered that anyone would be interested in his old-time gay activities. He sent McLeod a series of tapes describing his early activism, as well as a scrapbook of clippings and correspondence he had saved from the 1950s and 1960s that detailed his activism. McLeod in turn deposited them at the Canadian Lesbian and Gay Archives in Toronto.

This rediscovery of Egan set off a scholarly gold rush in Toronto, as his forgotten activities and the contents of his scrapbook opened up a lost world of 1940s through 1960s Canadian gay activism that had not been explored. Philip McLeod published a brief evaluation of Egan and the tabloids in the September 1986 issue of *Canadian Lesbian and Gay History Network Newsletter*[5]. This was followed by Robert Champagne's interview with Egan in *Rites* (December 1986 - January 1987), which led to his compilation *Jim Egan: Canada's Pioneer Gay Activist*, published in 1987[6]. Egan was interviewed by Gary Kinsman and was discussed in his *The Regulation of Desire*, published in 1987[7]. In the following years, Egan and Nesbit were interviewed by others as their court challenge gained more public attention. David Churchill undertook a video interview of Jim and Jack in 1990 as part of his research for his master's thesis entitled "Coming Out in a Cold Climate: A History of Gay Men in Toronto during the 1950s," completed in 1993[8]. David Adkin was introduced to the Egan papers at the Canadian Lesbian and Gay Archives and decided to do a documentary film recounting both the early days of Jim's activism in Toronto and the court challenge, then under way. The result was "Jim Loves Jack: The James Egan Story," released in 1996[9]. Most recently, Jim and Jack appeared as one of the couples featured in Michael Riordon's book *Out Our Way: Gay and Lesbian Life in the Country*, published in 1996[10].

Although there are now numerous writings on Jim and Jack, as well as a film, none has provided sufficient detail to satisfy my curiosity about Jim Egan's early activism. Some contradictions have also crept into published accounts of Egan's life. I have undertaken the present work in an attempt to provide a more detailed portrait of Jim Egan's early activist years. This work explores the question of

Egan's background and early sexual identity, his voracious appetite for learning (mostly self-directed), and the influence of wartime experiences on his sexual development. It is concerned particularly with examining the social and personal circumstances that allowed Jim Egan to become Canada's earliest known public gay activist.

A Note on Sources and Methodology

I have taken an unusual approach in compiling this book. I decided that the best way to tell Jim Egan's story would be for him to tell it himself, in his own words. One characteristic stands out in the Egan interviews I've seen in print and on screen and in our own conversations. Jim Egan is a talker. He is eloquent and opinionated. So, this work is in fact an oral history of Jim Egan, as told by Egan and compiled and edited by Don McLeod. With Egan's permission, and with the permission of the interviewers, I have compiled a narrative of Egan's life, using his own words, from a series of taped interviews conducted over a period of ten years. I have incorporated elements from the audiotapes Egan sent to Philip McLeod in 1986, from the videotape of Egan and Nesbit done by David Churchill in 1990, and from three hours of audiotape memoirs sent to me by Egan in 1996. In addition, I taped telephone interviews with Egan twice in 1996 and have corresponded with him by mail. I examined the Egan accessions at the Canadian Lesbian and Gay Archives, and have undertaken extensive research at the Metropolitan Toronto Reference Library. I have tried to verify every fact that Egan revealed in the interviews, and have made slight editorial changes and corrections where required. Finally, I sent a draft of the work to Jim and Jack, so that they could read the text and make comments or corrections.

A few words of caution before we proceed with Jim Egan's story. This memoir is written from a gay male perspective and includes some of Jim Egan's personal biases. It should be seen as the experience of one man only, and is best summed up in one of Egan's comments to me:

> The opinions that I have about what gay life was like in Toronto in the 1940s through the mid-1960s are definitely my own. I don't pretend to speak on behalf of the gay community. I am sure there are other gay men who lived there at the same time who have an altogether different view of what it was like to be gay in Toronto during this period. At

that time I was totally self-accepting as a gay man. I thought that being gay was simply wonderful. I couldn't see anything wrong with it, and at no time in my life did I ever wonder what it would be like to try to change and become heterosexual. The thought never entered my mind! And I was convinced, as far as gay rights were concerned, that I was right and society was wrong. There was never a doubt in my mind about that. So it was on that basis that I saw the world. My world view was an unusual one for the time.

Don McLeod
Toronto, August 1998

Chapter One: Beginnings

I was born at St. Michael's Hospital in Toronto on 14 September 1921, which makes me a Virgo. My parents were living at 281½ George Street at the time. My father, James Egan, was a big, easy-going Irishman, and although he'd been born in Toronto he was Irish to the core; the family was from County Tyrone. He worked as a fine cabinet maker for the Gerhard Heintzman piano company, making piano cases — the wooden portion of the piano — which in those days were all done by hand, including the staining and all the finish. My mother, Nellie (Josephine) Engle, had been raised mostly in Monte Carlo.

My parents married late in life, especially for those days. Father was fifty-six when I was born, and Mother was forty-one, I believe. One year and two months after I arrived, my brother, Charles, was born. As things turned out, Charles was gay also. Like many gay men I have known down through the years, we were born of parents who married late in life. Whether this had anything to do with our sexual orientation, I don't know. I strongly suspect it didn't, but it is rather interesting considering the number of gay men I've known who came from a similar situation.

I have nothing but the happiest memories of my childhood. We moved to 39 Westlake Avenue, in east-end Toronto, when I was about three years old. I have vague recollections of Westlake Avenue and they all tend to run together. But one of the things I do remember particularly is the nearby Danforth Creamery [at 1396 Danforth Avenue]. I remember my dad and I going up there and sitting at the counter in the dairy, and for a nickel you could have all the buttermilk you could drink.

My first real memory of childhood that I can pinpoint would be when I was approximately eight years old and we moved from Westlake Avenue to 245 Bain Avenue, between Carlaw and Pape avenues. We had only recently moved, and I remember sitting on the front steps watching about seven or eight of the boys on the street playing what we called kick the can. And I can remember, even at that young age, thinking, "What a bunch of louts. Why are they wasting their time and energy kicking a can up and down the street?"

My dad was very fond of walking. When I was young he and I would walk for miles on a Saturday in Toronto. We'd very often walk from Bain Avenue to the St. Lawrence Market. I had a great

Josephine Egan with Jim, ca. 1923.

Josephine Egan with Charles and Jim Egan, ca. 1928.

Jim and Charles Egan, ca. 1928.

relationship with him, although he died when I was fourteen, and because of that it was what I suppose you'd call a limited relationship.

When I was about nine years old he took me up to the Don River to visit a famous swimming hole there. It was known as the Clay Banks — although some referred to it as Bare Ass Beach — and it had been popular with the young men of Toronto for God only knows how long. My dad had learned to swim there when he was a boy, in the 1870s. We went up there one Saturday to teach me to swim. There I found myself surrounded by about a hundred naked young men. I realize, thinking back on it, that while I was not exactly sexually attracted to them, I felt an undefined excitement. It was at the Clay Banks that I first caught sight of pubic hair, which fascinated me and which I would come to find highly erotic throughout my life.

I was extremely fortunate compared with some young gay males. Mind you I'm not saying I had any intimations of being gay at the age of nine. I didn't. But I certainly had that feeling that many gays have that I was somehow different than the other boys. I had only the faintest notion of that, but I did feel different. I felt somewhat alienated from them, but I was fortunate in that I was never what could be described as a sissy. I got along quite well with the other boys on the street. We chummed around together. But they were interested, eventually, in playing baseball and I never, ever, had the faintest interest in that sort of thing. And so it developed, in a perfectly natural way, that I became very much of a loner, which didn't bother me in the least. I didn't miss their company. I could have joined in, and if I'd been willing to play baseball I would have been welcome. But I was not willing, and I was never one to go along with the herd. I didn't require association with them enough to inconvenience myself and waste time, as I saw it.

It was partly because of being on my own, but at some point, by the time I was eleven or twelve, I began to read. At the beginning I didn't read a great deal, but I did read far more than any of the boys on the street, whom I don't think ever read anything. By the time I was about fourteen I was an absolutely omnivorous reader. Everything was grist to the mill! I couldn't get enough of it. Now, my father was not an intellectual man — I don't recall seeing him ever read a book. My mother read a bit of Dickens and the *Rubaiyat of Omar Khayyam*, but other than that she was not a reader. I was very lucky in the sense that my mother, who became the dominant force in my life after my father died, never questioned my reading. Although, if I ever wanted to talk about what I was reading and express some interest to her about it, she was always a willing listener.

When I was around twelve to fourteen years old I used to buy copies of my two favorite English boys' magazines. One was called *The Magnet*, and the other was called *The Gem*. And then there was *The Boy's Own Annual*. Although there was never a whisper of homosexuality in them, looking back now it seems that the stories in these publications were charged with homoerotic implications. I can remember so much of them, so clearly, all these many years later. Especially stories from *The Magnet*. Harry Wharton, who was the head of the Remove, and his best friend Bob Cherry. Dr. Quelch, who was the form master, and Dr. Locke, who was the dean of Greyfriars School. I read these stories religiously. The schoolboys who were depicted in them were probably sixteen or seventeen years old, and were shown in line drawings of idealized youthful beauty. I suppose I projected a degree of friendship that probably wasn't there. But, of course, we know now that English boarding schools always had been hotbeds of homosexuality. And although, as I said, the matter was never mentioned in the stories, it seems to me that it would be very easy to interpret the stories that way. And, believe me, my imagination went wild!

I gradually became an omnivorous reader. A lot of my reading was not necessarily intellectual. I read everything by H. Rider Haggard and Conan Doyle and Verne and Dickens and most of H.G. Wells. I read all the Saint stories by Leslie Charteris, the Charlie Chan books, Agatha Christie, the Ellery Queen books, Erle Stanley Gardner, and everything that Edgar Rice Burroughs ever wrote. And many biographies and autobiographies. I used to buy the old *Doc Savage* and *The Shadow* magazines every month. I also became very interested in poetry, and I read a wide range of poets — Kipling, A.E. Housman, Whitman (one of my favorites), Poe, the sonnets of Shakespeare, and so on. I simply gobbled up books in the library, at the corner of Danforth and Pape avenues.

As I became aware of my own interest in males, I found that in those days, of course, there were very few references to homosexuality in any of these books. There was Whitman, when I finally discovered him, and Housman, whom I discovered when I was sixteen or seventeen, but even then I still knew very, very little. I had a vague idea that there was some sort of a gay world out there, but I knew nothing whatever about it. I don't know how life was for other kids. We're talking here about Toronto in the late 1930s, and in my experience boys were a lot more innocent in those days than they are today. But, for some reason or other, by the time I came across Housman's *A Shropshire Lad* and *More Poems*, reading through those poems I had the distinct impression that he was talking about what I felt. I found some of them to be absolutely heartbreaking.

The work that really triggered gay awareness for me was my quite accidental discovery of *The Picture of Dorian Gray*, by Oscar Wilde. And although I was probably fifteen when I read that book I instantly recognized myself as Basil Hallward. I was puzzled by Lord Henry Wotton, whom I thought was the same, but since he was married I couldn't quite figure that out. It didn't take long to understand that most gay men in the 1890s did get married. They were obligated to by society. And, as in the case of Lord Henry, it was clearly a marriage of convenience. Then I was puzzled by the fact that Dorian allegedly fell in love with Sibyl Vane, but it was sometime later when I realized that she was just another pretty ornament that he would add to his string of possessions, like jewels and incense and tapestries and such. When I figured that much out, I then decided that I would have to find out who this man Oscar Wilde was. In those days it was difficult to find very much. There were books written about him, but they were all so carefully veiled.

When I was about twelve or thirteen years old, living next door to us, at 247 Bain Avenue, was an older English couple, Mr. and Mrs. Ethelbert Wright. They had three or four children, all of whom died young. The last one, Buster, died of leukemia when he was seventeen. I already had the hots for Buster, although Buster hardly knew I existed. But Mr. and Mrs. Wright more or less took me under their wing, for some reason. I guess I became a surrogate son to them and began to spend a lot of time next door. Mr. Wright worked as a paper cutter and, although he was relatively uneducated, he had educated himself in certain areas that interested him. One of his passions was lepidoptery. He had acquired a huge collection of moths and butterflies and beetles, and I became very much interested in this, also. I began to develop such a collection myself, eventually ending up with hundreds of specimens.

By the time I was thirteen or fourteen I realized that I was sexually attracted to males. I'd never heard the words "gay" or "homosexual." I think it must be difficult for someone today to believe that young fellows then had never heard these words, but it was certainly true in my case and amongst the boys I knew in working-class, east-end Toronto. Although I didn't know these words, I sure knew what I liked. I became sexually active with some of the boys on the street. Contrary to what has been said about me, that "at the age of thirteen Jim Egan was picking up boys on the streets of Toronto," nothing could be further from the truth. The fact is that there were six or eight boys on the street about my own age, give or take a few months. And when I was thirteen, somehow or other, I haven't the foggiest remembrance of how it all got started, we started sexual experimentation with each other. It was no more than what that arch-hypocrite Lord Alfred Douglas described as "the usual schoolboy nonsense," which he alleged was all that ever happened between he and Oscar Wilde. But certainly it was nothing more than the usual schoolboy nonsense for me at the age of thirteen.

One of the things I quickly discovered with these kids was that while they all liked to fool around, they certainly didn't want to talk about it. And I realized early on that it was something that could not be discussed, but it was a fun thing and you could do it anytime the opportunity arose. One of the factors that contributed to this experimentation among schoolboys was the fact that girls were not sexually active. In those days the typical girl had been thoroughly brainwashed by her mother, and society in general, into believing that her only hope for any kind of a life was to trap a husband, to become a wife and mother. The bait in the trap was her virginity. Now, these girls would giggle and squeal and shriek and flirt and allow a boy to squeeze their ass, perhaps, but that's as far as it went. The whole social scene was entirely different from today.

So, by the time the boys got to be about fifteen they suddenly discovered girls and to my absolute incredulity it appeared that they would rather hang around with this gaggle of screeching, screaming, giggling, pimply virgins than fool around in the garage or in the nearby empty house. And I just learned to accept that. I didn't understand it. I wasn't interested in the girls at all, and never would be. In fact, I later began to think that I must be a positively unique gay man because, having started off with an awareness of my homosexual orientation at thirteen years old, I cannot ever recall having a conscious romantic or sexual interest in any female in my entire life. That doesn't mean I haven't enjoyed women's company —

I've always had many women friends, both lesbian and straight. But many of the gay men I've known have passed through a phase where they were either married or engaged or divorced or whatever. Also, for whatever reason, and I have no explanation for it, I never spent so much as ten seconds agonizing over the fact that I was attracted to other males. I spent a lot of time *looking* for other males, but I certainly wasn't worried about it. For some reason I just took the whole thing in my stride as though that's the way it was, and I came to the conclusion that since I felt that way about other males there obviously must be other guys in the world who felt the same way as I did. As events subsequently demonstrated, I was quite correct. I found perhaps not more than I needed but a reasonable number so that I had lots of contacts, even when I was a kid.

I suspect now, looking back on it, that ninety percent of those contacts were with boys who were simply horny kids. They were not gay. And, indeed, I went back to the old street, Bain Avenue, where I grew up, when I was about twenty-five years old. I just took part of a day and wandered down there and walked around and looked the old place all over. It hadn't changed a scrap. One of the boys that I had fooled around with on more than one occasion was sitting on his front doorstep, and I walked over and said, "Hi, how are you? You must be Jack." And he said, "Yes, I am." I was wearing a beard by that time and so I said, "I'm Jim Egan. Do you remember me?" And he said, "Oh, yea, sure." So we sat down and talked. I just casually asked, you know, where's Bill, and where's Allan, and where are the rest, and named them all. They were all married and were all parents by this time. So, fooling around, which was fairly extensive, certainly didn't hurt any of them as far as their heterosexual development was concerned. As for myself, by the time I got to be thirteen, as I say, I realized that I was more or less in a category by myself and I gradually developed into very much of a loner. I had nothing in common with the kids on the street, beyond a little fooling around, and they all began to acquire a great interest in sports, which never interested me at all. Except, I might say that Withrow Park had a large playing field and every Saturday there were lacrosse games. And in those days the changing rooms were open. Many of the spectators used to wander in and talk to the players. The players were all around eighteen or nineteen years old and I tell you I was there like iron filings to a magnet, watching all these drooly boys take off their clothes and put on their jockstraps, and so on. There were absolutely no inhibitions amongst them at all. They wandered around stark naked, and I found it a most attractive place and went back after the game was over. So I would sit through this dreary lacrosse game in order to enjoy the visions in the changing room!

I'm not sure how old I was when I started school. My mother was a convert to Catholicism, and like all converts was a far more zealous Catholic than many Catholics born to the faith. So I was enrolled in the separate school Holy Name, which was at 690 Carlaw Avenue, just south of Danforth Avenue. There I acquired a life-long aversion to formal education. I was taught by a gaggle of desiccated virgins known as the Sisters of St. Joseph, the most miserable, vicious, venomous collection of females I think I ever met. I was a rotten, poor student and how I ever got through any of the grades during my years at school I will never know. I loathed and despised every minute of it. But, nevertheless, I managed to graduate from that school when I was fourteen.

I was never a devout Catholic. My father was anything but devout, but would obediently tag along to church on Sunday with Mother and my brother and myself. Mother didn't worry too much, I think, about the nitty gritty details of Catholicism. In broad terms, she was a devout Catholic. She went to confession, she went to Holy Communion, and she saw to it that we were baptised and confirmed and the rest of it. But by the time I was fifteen, and after my experience with the Sisters of St. Joseph, I had decided that the entire theology was absolute hogwash and I wanted nothing to do with it whatever. For a short while after I obediently went to church, to please Mother, but not for long. This does not mean that I did not develop strong spiritual beliefs later on.

It was now 1936 and time to go to high school. By then I had an overwhelming urge to be a doctor. I went through *Gray's Anatomy* and read a good portion of it, and I read another book dealing with physiology. The problem was, although I didn't know it at the time, I realize that my mother must have applied for welfare, because money was in short supply. Obviously, with my father dead, and with the Depression at its height, I had to make a decision about going to school. Well, what I wanted to do, of course, was go to high school and obtain grade thirteen (called senior matriculation in those days), which would have enabled me to go on to medical school. But I soon realized that my dream of becoming a doctor was an absolute impossibility. There were no bursaries or grants or scholarships or loans in those days. The only way I could have gone to medical school would have been to go to school and get myself a job at the same time. And I didn't have sufficient confidence in myself that I would be able to do my studies and at the same time hold down a job.

So, ever the pragmatist, I decided to go to the Eastern High School of Commerce and take a course in typing, bookkeeping, relatively simple mathematics, and so on. A general commercial course. I was never so bored in my life with the whole first year that I was there. It was just excruciating. We had only two teachers of ability. One was a Mr. Ward, who taught a class that was a mixture of physics, biology, and chemistry. It was a very superficial science course and I did very well in it because I was keenly interested in what we were doing. And my favorite class was English literature, taught by Mr. Chelsea Rowe. If you can imagine parents inflicting a name such as Chelsea on a son, especially in those days! I didn't think about it at the time, but looking back I realize that Chelsea Rowe was a dear old queen who lived in a state of perpetual frustration because most of the young clods in the class had no more interest in English literature than I had in learning to speak Swahili. I, on the other hand, was his absolute favorite, because I had a supplementary reading list that was pages long. But the consequence of that supplementary reading list was that I failed my first year dismally, except in English literature and in the science class. So I decided, all right, I'll repeat, and this time I will put my mind to it and really try to get through this thing. However, I went back and at the end of two months I just realized that this was not for me.

That takes care of my so-called education. Whatever education I may have I acquired entirely on my own through extensive reading. Most of my reading was quite random. But then one day, while I was walking down Bain Avenue, this little Scotswoman named Mrs. Burns scuttled off the veranda when she saw me carrying these books and she inquired what I was reading. She gave me the best advice that anybody ever gave me in my life, and for which I will be eternally grateful. She said, "Read everything you can get your hands on. While you're reading, have a pad and a pencil beside you and a dictionary, and every time you come to a word and you don't know the meaning, look it up in the dictionary and write it down. If you go to the library and you search for something to interest you, and you can't find anything that you're really interested in, just take a book off the shelf. It doesn't matter what the book is, just take it home and read it, and learn new words and learn how to speak."

During this time I had an uncle by marriage, Wilbur Jewison, who'd married my father's sister Maggie. His roots were in Marmora, Ontario, which is in the Peterborough district. After Maggie died and he retired from Bell Telephone in Toronto, Wilbur purchased a home in a small village called Bailieboro, and remarried. And as there was little work in Toronto in 1937, he suggested that I come out there, and that with his connections — he knew everyone for miles around — he would get me a job working on a family farm. And so, I did. At the age of sixteen I left Toronto and went out to Bailieboro, and I stayed there working on family farms until I was almost eighteen. I was wiry and strong in those days. My experience on the farm was one I will always cherish. I always loved working on the farm, doing general work such as ploughing, bringing in the hay, the silage, milking cows, feeding the pigs — all those things.

Jim Egan, ca. 1936.

Charles and Jim Egan, 1937.

Chapter Two: Wartime and After: Gaining Gay Experience

A few months before I turned eighteen I was involved in a relatively minor automobile accident. I'd learned to call square dances and was in great demand in the Peterborough area. This young fellow and I were coming back from a dance one night in his father's car and we ran into a great Clydesdale horse that had broken out of the pasture. In those days, water was put into the radiator of the car through the cap ornament at the front of hood. When we hit the horse the ornament was smashed, broke loose, and came through the windshield. As a result I got a sliver of glass in my left eye that resulted in a corneal scar.

Canada declared war on Germany on 10 September 1939, less than two weeks before my eighteenth birthday. I came down to Toronto shortly after I turned eighteen and wanted to join the Army. By this time I was developing itchy feet like you wouldn't believe. I had no idea that I would ever want to settle down anywhere. I had read all of Richard Halliburton's books and books on soldiers of fortune and travel and beating your way around the world. When I went to enlist I was acceptable to them except for the corneal scar. In those days, with the war just nicely under way, they were taking only those men who were in A-1 condition. They agreed that I could join the Army if I had an operation to remove the corneal scar. Well, I didn't even know this scar was there and I had no intention of allowing anyone to fool around and try to remove it, since it really wasn't a problem. I refused, and was given a discharge, which meant I was absolutely free from call-up to the Army.

During this time I had been reading a great deal about medicine. I also became quite interested in natural history and read voluminously on that subject. I realized that I was going to have to get a job of some kind. Of course, most of the able-bodied men were heading off to war and plenty of job opportunities were coming available. So, with my interest in medicine and natural history, I applied for a job as departmental technician with the University of Toronto Department of Zoology. Although I certainly didn't have the qualifications and experience, they were so desperate for someone that they hired me.

In my new position I taught myself all I needed to know as I went along. I embalmed rabbits and preserved frogs. I learned a technique in which the blood systems of these animals are injected with red latex in the arteries, and blue in the veins. When the latex sets (like a rubber band) it enables the student, when dissecting the animal, to distinguish arteries from veins. I also had a large lab at my disposal and learned to make microscope slides. Eventually, I churned out hundreds of slides of nerve, muscle, and brain tissue.

After spending about a year at the University of Toronto I went to the Connaught Laboratories, which was virtually next door. I worked in the insulin production department, which was little more than a factory job. There was nothing very scientific about it. I found it to be a mechanical business and rapidly became fed up. Then, one day, a tall, distinguished gentleman showed up. Nobody knew who he was, but he was wandering around all over the labs. He engaged me in conversation and asked me some general questions, and then away he went. The next thing I knew, he asked that I be posted to him as an assistant.

At this time there was a dreadful shortage of typhus vaccine, which was required for the war effort. As far as I remember, there was none being produced in Canada. So it was decided that Dr. Raymond Parker, the tall, distinguished gentleman, would come up to Toronto and open a laboratory within the Connaught Labs to develop a method for producing typhus vaccine. This involved an awful lot. I didn't realize what I was getting myself into. Dr. Parker was a brilliant man in his field[1]. He had worked for years in virology at the Rockefeller Institute for Medical Research, in New York, and had studied under the great Alexis Carrel[2]. But Dr. Parker wasn't a very practical person. So much of the practical end of the work fell on me. I'm not complaining about it, because I enjoyed it. Ultimately, over a period of time, we developed a method of producing the vaccine, and perfected the method. Once that was done we moved on to other research. Dr. Parker was interested in pursuing his tissue culture experiments. He'd written the book *Methods of Tissue Culture* and wanted to pursue cancer research using tissue culture methods[3]. I got to work with him on that for awhile. Soon another man, Dr. J.W. Fisher, came into the lab, because it was far too big a space for the amount of work we were doing. At that time the poliomyelitis epidemic was rampant in Toronto, and one of the things they wanted to determine was if it was possible for houseflies to transmit the polio virus. We went through quite a few experiments and determined that indeed the housefly could transmit polio.

Eventually I had a disagreement with Dr. Parker, and I decided that I would leave[4]. And I did, and that is when I joined the merchant navy. This time they weren't so concerned about my eye. I joined up in 1943, for approximately the last two years of the war.

The first ship I was on was a Norwegian ship under British registry, the *Konge Sverre*. I worked as an ordinary seaman and made something like a hundred and forty dollars a month. There was no overtime pay, and I almost died from the amount of fish I had to eat. I was on the *Konge Sverre* for a year and two months, and for the last three or four months I practically lived on bread and peanut butter, because I couldn't face another piece of fish.

On my maiden voyage we left New York City with a load of wheat, destined for Bari, Italy. The war had just barely ended in Italy. We threaded our way through the harbour at Bari, through all the half-submerged shipwrecks, only to find that the unloading equipment had been damaged. Ordinarily the wheat would be unloaded through great suction vacuums, but they had all been smashed to pieces from the bombing. So the wheat had to be unloaded by hand, which was a tremendous job and took several weeks. As a result I had a great opportunity to visit Bari and other towns in the vicinity.

Most of the guys I knew in the merchant navy were nice people, but sometimes a bit rough around the edges. Generally at night everyone would go ashore, and someone would ask, "Are you going to go ashore tonight, Jim?" And I'd say, "No, I don't think so." And I didn't. I didn't want to go ashore with those fellows at all because, even though I enjoy drinking, I don't drink the way they drank. I couldn't keep up with them in the bars, and there would be no pleasure for me. So I'd say I was going to read, and I'd stay on board ship until all the guys had gone who were going ashore, and then I'd go ashore by myself. And after I'd said no maybe twice, they didn't ask me any more. They just picked up that I wasn't interested in going ashore with them.

Members of the crew were quite often hard-drinking heterosexuals with limited interests. It didn't matter where we were, and it didn't matter what there was to see, all most of them ever did was hit the first bar, load up, get blind drunk, and then head to the nearest whorehouse. And that was it! They did this every night they went ashore. It came to be quite a joke. On the morning we were to set sail, the crew would show up on the ship and they'd all have terrible hangovers as they'd really put on a load of booze the night

Jim peeling potatoes in the merchant navy,
ca. 1943.

before. By the next day everyone had sobered up again, and they'd all sit around and say, "What a lousy hole that was. Shit, I'd never want to go back there again." And all they'd ever seen of the place was the first bar, and the nearest whorehouse!

On my own trips ashore I always dreaded running into them. I had a very awkward situation once in Bari. I walked into a trattoria there and sat down and was having a few drinks and suddenly realized there were a lot of female hookers around the place. They were drifting in and out. I suppose at that time there were thousands of Italian girls who had turned to prostitution because of conditions. I was just sitting there paying no attention and one or two of them wandered over to the table and I just shook my head, and they went away again. Suddenly five or six of the guys from the ship came in, and they saw me sitting there by myself. So they all came over and joined the table. Well, no sooner had they joined me than the place was surrounded by these hookers, who recognized that these guys were probably interested, even if I wasn't. I felt trapped. Under those circumstances, it's difficult to say no to a very attractive young Italian woman. There was a young woman who sat beside me, and when things started to break up and everyone left together I went with her. We got outside and I said, "Look, where do you live?" And she said, "Not too far from here." I asked her how much she charged, and I think I remember it was five thousand lire. So I said that I would go with her, and pay her the money, but I didn't want anything. She looked at me and said, "You are queer?" I asked how she knew. And she said, "I am just an ignorant girl, and about most things I know nothing. But about men, I know everything." I agreed to go with her, and she said, "Do not worry, I will say nothing." I followed her, and we walked into this big apartment block. Her mother and father and grandmother were there, and two or three brothers and sisters. They were all sitting around talking, and we walked straight through the room and into her bedroom. Everybody knew about it, but nobody said a word. I felt very embarrassed about the whole thing. So we slept together in the same bed, and had a good night's sleep. It probably did my reputation a world of good with the crew! That was my sole experience with a female, and that wouldn't have happened if I'd had my own way.

From Bari we went to Beirut, then to a place in Turkey called Iskenderun, and finally down through the Suez Canal. The *Konge*

Sverre was a tramp steamer, and we went from port to port to port.

Eventually we ended up in Sydney, Australia, and because I was a British subject I was allowed to pay off the ship. I then fulfilled the ambition of every merchant seaman in those days. Everybody wanted to get on an American ship because the wages and conditions were infinitely superior to those of other shipping lines. As opposed to a hundred and forty dollars a month, the lowest pay on the American ships was four hundred a month. In those days that was good money. As my next of kin, my mother received a free ten thousand dollar life insurance policy on me. There was full medical coverage for sickness or injury. Conditions on board were excellent — it was almost like travelling economy class today. And anyone who signed up on an American ship was eligible to join the American Seaman's Union upon returning to the States.

I served on American ships for the balance of the war, and also afterward. The one I remember best is the *Juan N. Seguine*, a Liberty Ship freighter. There were roughly thirty-five men in the crew, and six or eight officers.

The war was exciting and thrilling for me. I got to see a lot of the world — London, the Mediterranean, North Africa, Australia, the Philippines, New Guinea. I was very fortunate in that I was never sunk. We were dive bombed and chased by submarines. I spent a lot of time in New Guinea, when the Japanese were still at war with the Americans, and the Japanese would come over and drop bombs on or at the ship. This happened especially at Port Moresby, where the docking facilities were non-existent and we were anchored out in the bay.

As a young gay man, and one who was still very naive, it took me awhile to figure out that there was a real gay world out there. I eventually realized, of course, by going to places like London and Sydney, and Hamburg after the war, that there was an incredible gay underworld in all these places. And while I don't know what the legal situation was in many of them, the authorities closed a blind eye to it.

During the war the bars that were thought of as "gay" in these various ports were crammed every night of the week with Allied forces people. You'd see uniforms from every one of the Allied forces — Marines and sailors and Air Force — and ranks up to majors and colonels. Everyone was in uniform, and there was never any question of hassling those bars. They'd have decimated the Allied ranks if they had! The authorities simply closed an eye to it and allowed these places to operate. It was all very exciting.

There's a wonderful book by Allan Bérubé called *Coming Out Under Fire: The History of Gay Men and Women in World War Two*[5]. It tells about how so many young men who had been living in small towns or small cities were swept up in the draft. During the time they were living at home they knew of their feelings for other men, but they hadn't a clue as to what was going on. The war changed that, allowing them to see the world and meet others like themselves, sometimes in these bars. I also remember a book called *The Gallery*, by John Horne Burns[6]. One of the stories in it, "Momma," is set in a Neapolitan gay bar and gives a very good idea of the type of activities that went on in such places during or just after the war.

I remember when I was in London, sometime in 1944 or 1945. I went to Piccadilly Circus, which was one of the favorite cruising grounds, and met this young guy. We got into a conversation. He was obviously cruising, and so was I. We ended up in bed later on. He told me that when he was drafted into the Army he was so utterly frustrated because he knew he was gay and, being around all these guys in the barracks and the showers, he didn't know what to do about it. He didn't know where to go to meet other guys who had the same feelings.

At that time there was an organization called the U.S.O., run by the Americans, which had a huge centre in London called the Rainbow Corners. It was a place where servicemen could go for relaxation in the evening. They had pool tables, and desks with envelopes, and papers, and various games like cards, and so on. One of the things they did was give out tickets to all the big theatrical performances in London. So this boy was there one night and one of the women gave him a ticket to go to a variety show. At the show there was a stand-up comedian who made a comment about how thick the London fog was that night. He said, "It's almost as thick as the fairies in Piccadilly Circus." This boy's ears pricked up, and he thought, "Hmmm. Piccadilly Circus. Maybe that's where people like me meet." He went down there later and was only there for ten minutes before he met his first gay man and had his first gay experience. In its own way, this sort of remark served as an indirect liaison service for gay men. Of course, the comic didn't realize the service he was providing. But Piccadilly Circus was, at the height of the war, just fantastic!

I can't say, though, that I witnessed much gay activity on board ship. I did meet two guys on one American ship I suspected were gay. One of them didn't interest me in the least. The other one interested me greatly, but it was not a good idea to be known. I personally never experienced any hanky panky aboard ship. There was a Jamaican cook on one of my ships. He was gay and made no bones about it. But I don't think he had anything to do with any of the crew members. I remember that when we were in Italy there was an endless stream of cute young Italians in and out of the ship. They were all getting some sort of pay. You know, they weren't doing it because they were gay. In many of the places that we visited, especially shortly after the war, a very substantial percentage of young men were available. This was especially true in North Africa. You had to be careful, actually, in the outdoor cafés about looking at anybody too steadily for more than a split second, because they'd come right over to the table, and they'd be expecting a packet of cigarettes, and a cake of soap, and so on.

Right after the war I left the merchant navy, but only for a few months. I had two friends in Toronto, young guys about my own age who were both as straight as they come. They were interested in biology, too, and I suggested that the three of us get together and form a small biological supply company. And we did form the Ontario Biological Supply Company, but it didn't work. The company only survived about six months because the two of them were too carefree and irresponsible. They believed that self-employment meant only having to work when you felt like it. I found I was doing most of the work, and decided to join the merchant navy again.

Late in 1947 I decided to give up the merchant navy for good, and return to Toronto. I really loved life in the navy, but also realized that everyone I had met who'd been in it for many years was little more than a drunk. Some of them were really great guys — diamonds in the rough — but I was afraid of getting sucked into that way of life. I decided it was time to do something else.

Chapter Three: Living the Gay Life in Post-War Toronto

While I was in the merchant navy I didn't spend a great deal, so when I came back to Toronto in 1947 I had money in the bank. I lounged around for awhile before taking a job at a little restaurant called the Tea Pot Dome Tea Rooms [located below street level at 1 Adelaide Street East]. It was one of the popular gay spots for lunch. I heard about it, so I went down and applied for a job as kitchen helper.

I was curious about what is known as plastic fabrication. There were plants in Toronto that made, say, plastic ballpoint pens, and large plastic buttons for women's fur coats. At the time I was staying in a rooming house at 28-30 Grosvenor Street. There were a couple of other gay boys staying in the house, which was run by Mrs. Jane Gynn, a delightfully eccentric woman. One of the boys worked at this fabrication plant and said that I could get a job there easily. So I went down and applied for a job and got work immediately. I found it really very interesting for two or three months, but soon grew bored. I took these little jobs just for something to do. I certainly had no ambitions about being in the plastics or the restaurant business. It was a fill-in. At that time I didn't have any particular ambition to do anything.

After I returned to Toronto I thought for the first time about investigating the local gay world. Apart from my experiences overseas in gay bars, I had not actively participated in the gay life. Of course, in the 1940s there were few places for gay men to meet in Toronto: a few parks, washrooms, several bathhouses, theatres, a few beverage rooms and restaurant hangouts, and private parties.

I had heard about the Savarin Hotel and a couple of other places. The local tabloid scandal sheets like *Flash*, *Hush Free Press*, and *Justice Weekly* sometimes mentioned the gay spots around town. But after I started going to the Savarin, to the Ford Hotel, and to the King Cole Room at the Park Plaza Hotel, I realized that while I still fully accepted that I was gay, and had no intention of even thinking of changing, I did not want to continue living what I would call a promiscuous life. I was never wildly promiscuous. I never went to the steam baths, not because I thought that there was anything wrong with it, but simply because that wasn't my idea of how to have sex. I decided that I wanted to meet another guy and settle down with him for the rest of my life.

The Savarin Hotel [located at 336-44 Bay Street] had the first gay

The Savarin Hotel, Toronto, ca. 1952. Photo by William E. Whittingham, Peake and Whittingham Ltd.

The beverage room, Savarin Hotel, Toronto, ca. 1952. Photo by William E. Whittingham, Peake and Whittingham Ltd.

beverage room I went to in Toronto. At that time it was one of the most popular gay spots in town. It was by no means exclusively gay, but a great many of the customers there were gay men. The bars were strictly segregated in those days — there were no women in the men's side. They were confined to the Ladies and Escorts side of the bar. And I noticed that the men would come in and so many of them would know each other. I hadn't observed that in the past. My previous experience in gay bars was to go in to pick someone up. I had reasonable success in that, but that was really the extent of my interest in them.

I gradually got to know other gay men who frequented the Savarin. And one night I walked in and my brother, Charles, was there, sitting with a table of shrieking faggots. This was the first time I knew he was gay. Charlie and I, when we were young, did not get along at all. I couldn't stand him, and I think he looked upon me as an intellectual snob. He was always scatterbrained and giddy. I don't think we ever discussed our gayness, it just gradually came to be accepted between us. Charlie was absolutely not interested in gay liberation; he'd say let's do it, not talk about it. Later on, I came to appreciate him. We used to go out and drink beer. Charlie had a tremendous sense of humour, and a capacity for beer like you wouldn't believe[1].

Early on, when I was coming into the gay world in Toronto, I shrank from overtly effeminate, queenly gay men. In my earlier experiences in gay places in Europe and the United States, though, I didn't mind them at all. It's funny when I stop and look back on it. Later on, I had many street queens as friends, and I loved them all.

In my attempts to find a steady partner I met probably three men that I was primarily madly in lust with. But I never actually fell in love with any of them. I don't believe in this expression "love at first sight." It may be true for some people, but it certainly isn't true for me. I don't see how I could ever fall in love with somebody with whom I did not have a lot in common. I might meet an attractive young man at a bar one night and after a little conversation we might end up in bed and have an apocalyptic night of it. But if in the morning he told me he was the Grand Imperial Wizard of the Ku Klux Klan, any thought of falling in love with him would have gone straight out the window. Mind you, this would not have interfered with the fact I was in lust with him, and I'd be perfectly willing to go back to bed. But there would be no thought in my mind of having a continuing relationship with him.

Well, one young man I met, who ended up committing suicide, was so good looking. I'd never seen anyone as good looking. He made a pass at me one night and we ended up in bed and had a wonderful time of it. But I knew perfectly well that any attempt to form a permanent relationship with him was doomed to failure. He was pursued constantly by older men and he could not resist flirtation. He simply wasn't made of the stuff that makes for being in a permanent relationship.

The other young man with whom I fell madly in lust would never, ever, admit that he was gay, although in my opinion he was as gay as I was. I knew it wouldn't work between us. And I had enough control over my emotions that I would never put myself into a position that would lead to a broken heart. That's what it would have amounted to.

It was in the Savarin that I first met Jack Nesbit. When I went there quite often I'd see a man called Dick Nelson. He was at least fifteen years older than me. Dick was a nice guy, but we had no physical interest in each other. Sometimes he'd be sitting alone and I'd go over and join him. He was quite a reader, too, and we'd sip beer and talk about books. Dick gave me the first explicitly gay novel that I ever read, Gore Vidal's *The City and the Pillar*[2]. We'd also sit there and eyeball the young stuff coming into the Savarin. We were both interested in the guys twenty to twenty-two years old. Dick knew some of them, and I gradually got to know a few of them, too.

One night we were sitting there admiring the young men and Jack Nesbit and Larry Rowdon came in. Jack and Larry were what you would call "sisters," as the saying was in those days. They went out together in the evening for beers. Jack had met Dick, this friend of mine, so when they passed the table Dick said, "Hi, Jack. How are you?" Jack came over, and Dick introduced me to Jack and I fell instantly in lust. I was smitten with Jack!

About two weeks later I decided to go out to have a beer and I went to the King Cole Room at the Park Plaza Hotel. It was about evenly split gay and straight, with a lot of students from the University of Toronto. On that night Jack was sitting in the King Cole Room with three or four other gay men. He'd been drinking quite a bit and was feeling no pain, as the saying goes. Jack saw me sitting further down in the bar and sort of beckoned to me. I picked up my glass and went to join them at the table. Then Jack said something like, "I've been asking all these guys if they want to go steady with me, and none of them will. How about you? Would you like to go steady with me?" Ever the pragmatist, I replied, "Now just a minute. This is rather sudden. Maybe we ought to get to know each other better first."

Well, we made a date to meet the next night, and I don't remember what we did. We started to go out together for long walks, and I think we went to a couple of the Promenade concerts. We found that we had interests in common, and on 23 August 1948 we made a commitment to each other. Although we didn't know it at the time, as things turned out we had more in common than we realized, which helped us to be a successful gay couple. For one thing, at that time neither of us had much money. I was down to a few dollars in my bank account, and Jack had about thirty dollars in his. Neither of us, we discovered, was the slightest bit interested in style or fashion or fancy clothes, as many gay men were. This meant nothing to us at all. We also recognized fairly early on in the relationship that we both dreamed of owning our own home outright, without a mortgage on it. In order to accomplish that, we were prepared to work hard and economize. Finally, we were lucky in that we had no family problems. My mother had spent time as a young woman in Monte Carlo, and had known gay people. Shortly after I met Jack I decided I should tell her I was gay. Mother never turned a hair. Her only comment was, "As long as you're happy, dear, that's the only thing that's important." When I brought Jack home for the first time, she took to him like another son and they had a wonderful relationship for as long as she lived.

Within a few weeks of meeting Jack I moved in with him. Jack's parents managed the Cotswold Court Apartments [at 164 Cumberland Street, near the University of Toronto]. Jack and I lived there in a two-room suite downstairs. Jack's parents were, in the kindliest sense of the word, simple people. They treated me like another son. I think they may have had some vague understanding of the nature of my relationship with Jack, but I don't know for sure that they exactly understood what was going on. I do remember one night, though, driving them out for dinner. Jack and I had been together for three or four years. At some point, right out of the clear blue sky, Mrs. Nesbit spoke up from the back seat and said, "You know, now I can die happy because Jack's found someone who can look after him." And that was all that was said about it, but it seemed to me to indicate that she had some idea about what was going on.

When I met Jack he was twenty-one and was working at the Provincial Audit Office at Queen's Park as a Clerk Group Three office boy. Jack was always interested in hairstyling, and while we were still living on Cumberland Street he quit this job and took a course in professional hairstyling. For a number of years after, Jack would run his own hairstyling business and would on occasion manage other people's shops.

During my time at the University of Toronto in the early 1940s, preparing biological specimens, I had come into contact with a man by the name of Troyer. He operated a one-man biological supply business, collecting and preserving biological specimens for schools and universities. One night in the summer of 1949 Mr. Troyer showed up at our apartment on Cumberland Street. His business was expanding and he couldn't handle the work alone. He offered me a job at his place, which was at Oak Ridges, about fifteen miles north of Toronto. With the job went a small house, immediately adjacent. I talked it over with Jack and we decided we'd leave Toronto. By this time we were getting pretty well fed up with the gay world there. Between us we had dozens of gay friends, and in those days there were parties every weekend. I don't know how we survived as a couple in that atmosphere, but we did[3].

Late in 1949 we moved up to Oak Ridges. We continued to see a fair few friends, as it was only a few miles north of Toronto and it made for a nice Sunday afternoon drive. But we gradually stopped seeing many of them because most of the gay people we knew did not want to live as Jack and I did. The idea of living in the country was anathema to them. But it was great for us, and it gave us an opportunity to have the first home of our own.

Jack Nesbit and Jim Egan, ca. 1949.

The house at Oak Ridges, Ontario.

Christmas dinner at Oak Ridges, 1949.

Jim and Jack at Oak Ridges, 1954.

Chapter Four: Challenging the Conspiracy of Silence: Jim Egan's Emergence As a Gay Activist during the 1950s

Toronto could be a dangerous place for gay men during the late 1940s and 1950s. Police entrapment was always a serious threat for the many men who went cruising. Every once in a while there would be a crackdown on "sexual perversion," and all the activities at the theatres and parks and other gay cruising areas would come under scrutiny. The washrooms at High Park became a regular police target. The police might concentrate on one area, say High Park, and then swoop down on other places, such as Philosopher's Walk at the University of Toronto, the Honey Dew Coffee Shop [at 321 Yonge Street], or the Rio Theatre [at 373 Yonge Street][1].

Sometimes the police used their younger recruits as bait. The police cadets were of legal age but looked about eighteen years old, and they'd dress in skintight blue jeans and drop around to the most popular cruising spots of the day. They would sprawl out on a park bench, and call out a friendly "Hi, how are you tonight," to any man who passed. I need scarcely say that this was an open invitation to a gay man to stop and chat. If things didn't move quickly enough, the young man might then stretch out and rub his crotch and say, "Oh, man, am I ever feeling horny tonight." Well, that's all it took. As soon as the gay man laid a hand on him, bang, he was arrested and charged with committing an act of gross indecency. I talked with several gay men who were trapped in this manner. In some cases the cadet was feeling horny and allowed the gay man to give him a blow job, only to arrest him later. Once the gay man was charged and hauled into court, there was absolutely nothing he could say in his own defence. For him to tell the court that this young man had agreed to a sexual encounter would have seemed unbelievable. And so they were always convicted. The penalty was usually a fine of about a hundred dollars. The real danger in conviction was having your name, age, and sometimes even occupation and address printed in the local scandal sheets, which were always interested in publishing news of local "sex crimes." Papers like *Hush Free Press* and *Justice Weekly* delighted in covering the "disgusting sex orgies" of members of the "limp-wrist set," or the "knothole club." Publication of one's name in such an article was an unmitigated disaster, especially for those men who were closeted or married[2].

I think the majority of gay men that I knew in Toronto during the late 1940s and 1950s were reasonably content with their lot. While there was no such thing as a gay rights or gay liberation movement at the time, this really didn't matter to most of them. Toronto just wasn't the sort of place then where many gays would have supported an organized gay rights group. Most gay men at the time did have to keep their sexuality hidden from family, friends, and the boss, but as long as that was done there were places to meet, places to cruise, and so on. And if you were unable to accept the fact you were gay, and you wanted to stay in the closet, it was relatively simple to do so. In those days, members of straight society generally didn't have a clue about gay people. Two men going to rent an apartment almost never ran into problems because it would never occur to the landlord that they might be a gay couple. So, although there was a homophobic social climate during this period that cried out for change, I think it's important to note that the situation was not entirely bad.

After the war there was increasing mention of homosexuality in the mainstream press. This was no doubt influenced by the publication in 1948 of Dr. Alfred Kinsey's *Sexual Behavior in the Human Male*[3], as well as popular novels with gay content such as Gore Vidal's *The City and the Pillar* [1948]. I used to browse through the mainstream magazines and would often see articles on homosexuality. *Argosy*'s publication in August 1949 of Allen Churchill's "What Is a Homosexual?," with its sensational subheading "Here are the frank and startling facts of a plague which, according to Dr. Kinsey, has touched 37% of America's men," was a typical example[4]. Even though homosexuality was coming under the spotlight, it was almost always viewed as an abnormality or sickness. There were never any articles published from the gay point of view, which in my mind equalled a conspiracy of silence on the true nature of homosexuality.

Some of these articles were more outrageous than others. Take the example of Ralph H. Major Junior's "New Moral Menace to Our Youth," published in *Coronet* in September 1950. The preface to this article states that "Qualified editors and researchers spent six months collecting material, interviewing authorities, and evaluating information. The result is a significant survey of the entire subject as it endangers the youth of America ...." The article proceeds to discuss the supposed dangers posed by homosexuals preying on children, and supports its claims by quoting incredible comments made by public officials. For example, Eugene D. Williams, Special Assistant Attorney General of the State of California, is quoted as follows: "'All too often, we lose sight of the fact that the homosexual is an inveterate seducer of the young of both sexes, and that he presents a social problem because he is not content with being degenerate himself; *he must have degenerate companions, and is ever seeking younger victims* [emphasis his][5].'" This is the sort of thing that used to absolutely infuriate me. I would read something like that and I'd get so goddamned furious I would be inarticulate. This fury is what really prompted me to start writing letters to these publications in 1949, while we were at Oak Ridges, and which launched me on the road to public gay activism.

Today we may look back at Major's article and chuckle all the way through it. It's utterly hilarious, and I don't think any magazine would publish an article such as this today, except maybe the publications of the Ku Klux Klan or religious fringe groups. The mind boggles to think that such drivel could have ever been published! But, in 1949, when I started writing letters to combat this sort of thing, they were accepted as the norm and were published in influential mainstream magazines with wide distribution. Every time I saw one of these ridiculous articles, or a negative comment on homosexuality, I sat down at my old Underwood typewriter and did up a letter of complaint to the editor. Between 1949 and 1951 I sent letters to *Coronet, Esquire, Ladies' Home Journal, Parents' Magazine, Redbook, Time,* and other magazines[6]. None of the letters was published, but I think it was important that I sent them. For example, I sent a letter to *Time* in March 1951 in which I protested their use of the word "pervert" as a synonym for "homosexual." I simply let them know that there was at least one person out there who was not going to sit by and let them get away with what I considered to be gross inaccuracies and libels. At that time I had no knowledge of anyone else writing these sorts of letters or articles in Canada, certainly not in a sustained way. I thought it was important that someone do this, even if the letters had limited effect.

I was first published in a mainstream publication on 16 May 1950, when one of my letters appeared in the *Globe and Mail*[7]. The Kinsey Report was causing controversy in the press and I wrote to defend Kinsey in helping to bring sex into the modern age.

As I mentioned, at this time in Toronto there existed a number of tabloid newspapers that were popular scandal sheets. They were typically sixteen-page newsprint tabloids, published weekly, and were filled with gossip, reports of local crimes or scandals, local ads, and so on. They had names like *Flash, Hush Free Press, Justice Weekly*, and *True News Times*, and were really the predecessors of the trashy tabloids of today such as the *National Enquirer*[8]. Anyway, they quite often included a vituperative story about some unfortunate gay man who had been arrested or was charged with (as they used to delicately phrase it) "interfering with a Boy Scout," or something like that. I used to see these papers on the newsstand. I would pick them up and glance through them and would think how absolutely outrageous and unjust they were. So, I also started writing letters to the editors of these publications, and it was in the spring of 1950 that some of these began to be published in *Flash*.

For whatever reason, in May 1950 *Flash* published a long letter that I had written responding to a preposterous article entitled "Unparalleled Orgies of Perversion Exposed by Intrepid *Flash* Reporter," in which the reporter risked the dangers of one of Toronto's most notorious steam baths to report on all the sex he had seen there[9]. Oh, the article was heart-rending! My lengthy reply, which was entitled "Reader Defends Homos, Says They're Inverts," in turn caused several readers to write to attack my position[10]. This first publication of one of my letters opened the floodgates, and I threw myself into the cause.

I must say that when my letters started to be published I certainly didn't think it was because of any sympathy that the editors had for homosexuals or gay rights. I think it was the novelty of my point of view more than anything else that surprised and interested them. They wanted to stir up controversy. And I didn't mind the letters attacking me that came in from other readers. Most of them displayed an abysmal ignorance of homosexuality. They really didn't know what they were talking about. For example, when I complained about the injustice of the legislation of the day, no one ever actually replied "What injustice? The legislation is perfectly legitimate. It should be enforced." No, the replies were usually something silly like "How much longer are we going to be subjected to this filth from the pen of James Egan?," which I found more amusing than anything else.

In September 1950 I decided to try to write a book detailing the social and legal situation of homosexuals in various countries of the world. In order to do this I had to find copies of the penal codes of

P. O. Oak Ridges, Ontario.
May 6, 1950.

The Editor,
Globe and Mail,
140 King St., W.,
Toronto.

Dear Mr. Editor—
I would like to be permitted sufficient space in your paper
to reply to the letter of Wm. Gray regarding the review of the new Kinsey report.
When a book such as the Kinsey Report is published, it is
only natural that all intelligent and progressive people will want to know about it. Thus
it is part of the function of a newspaper to inform it's readers of the appearance of such
books. The more important the book, the more prominent should the book review be. In the
case of a book of such magnitude as the Report, the front page is the obvious choice for
the location of the review. One does not bury such reviews in the inside pages—these are
reserved for letters of the caliber of that of Mr. Gray's.
So you think the article was written to please a certain type
of moron, do you, Mr. Gray? I think they would have to be more than moronic if, after reading such a review they could think of nothing more intelligent to say than "so what".
I am sure that the good Dr. Kinsey would like to ask you
a few questions; you must have a rather peculiar mind. However, I imagine that he would no
doubt quickly join you and "give up hope".
The Kinsey Reports, apart from their scientific value to the
psychologist and psychiatrist (which is inestimable) for whom, of course they are chiefly
intended, are indicative of the progressive and intelligent approach which modern society
is adopting toward the subject of sex. Kinsey imagined much perhaps but tried to help bring
sex out of the Victorian wrappings which have stifled it for far too long. No subject is in
greater need of better understanding; but surrounded as it has been for years, with taboos
of all kinds, both social and religious, sex has been looked upon as something unclean
which "nice" people sturdily ignored. That it is at last being accepted as a part of the
life of everyone and is being sanely and seriously discussed is due in no small part to the
efforts of such men as Kinsey, Landau and Thornton. To many but three many
Mr. Gray represents the small minority who would return sex
to it's position of 50 years ago. Well Mr. Gray, it is here to stay so
you may as well accept the fact and try to like it. You can give up hope,
Yours very truly,

but you can't give up sex

Every kind

Vital

by means of the Reports, has done much to help bring

A draft of one of Egan's early letters to the *Globe and Mail,* 1950.

TRUE NEWS TIMES

10c NATIONAL EDITION

Vol. 13, No. 5   Monday, Feb. 4, 1952

GYPSY STEALS FROM WINNIPEGGER
Story on Page 5

QUEERS FLUSHED FROM 'LOVE' NEST

See Page 12

"PANSIES" BLOOM IN COCKTAIL BAR

At one time they made the Chez Paree their home-away-from-home but due to some diligent work on the part of the management they were weeded out and sent scurrying back to their nests. Maloney's Art Galleries and the Times Square Room of the King Edward Hotel played host at one time to a fair share of these masculine maidens.

However they have now apparently taken over the Nile Room of the Letros Tavern and on any Friday or Saturday night you could fire off a load of buckshot and very probably not hit a normal person. The "sweet things" sit around like animated mannequins, flutter their eyelashes, roll their eyes and slap each other playfully as they engage in a bit of gigglish repartee.

In general they behave very much like the Branksome Hall girls at a pink tea and they make no attempt to disguise their effeminate leanings. The ordinary citizen, by swallowing hard once in a while, can tolerate these obvious ones, but also mingled in the crowd are the sneaky perverts. This is the type who looks and acts masculine and usually prey on the young fellows.

These "Letros Ladies" are usually very well dressed and among them one finds "men" who are quite prominent in various professional circles in Toronto. A visit there is quite an eye-opener for the average citizen and don't think these "babes" don't kick and scratch when the chips are down.

Recently some normal guy took objection to having one of these queers engage his girl-friend in conversation and planted a fistful of fingers in his face. The high-pitched screams and shrieks that arose reminded one of the time the mouse ran rampant at the ladies' sewing circle. In all probability the pansy had not insulted the girl, but was merely enquiring as to her brand of perfume or whether she preferred the paste to the liquid deodorant. Then again he could have been objecting to the competition she afforded for a woman has no place among "its."

From "'Pansies' Bloom in Cocktail Bar," *Hush Free Press*, 17 March 1951, p. 6.

GIRL OF NINE ACCUSES MARRIED MAN OF 29

Justice WEEKLY

IMPRISON AND FINE MOLESTER OF YOUNG CHILDREN

Letters From All Over
On Spanking Down Under

10 cents

BEST WOODBINE RACE SELECTIONS

VOL. 11, No. 44   NATIONAL EDITION   November 3, 1956

HOMOSEXUAL ORGIES BRING MANY CONVICTIONS

(See Page 2)

SEXHIBITIONIST OF 18 BEING TREATED

the countries. During September and October I wrote a letter of inquiry to every foreign embassy in Ottawa, and received a considerable response. The more I thought about my proposed work, however, the more hesitant I became. I felt it might be a dull tome, somewhat on the scholarly side, and would not be of much interest to the average reader. And, with the appearance of Donald Webster Cory's *The Homosexual in America* in 1951, which was in some ways similar to what I hoped my own work would be, I decided to abandon the project[11].

In October 1950 a letter of mine was published for the first time in *True News Times*[12]. *TNT* published a ridiculous gay gossip or tid-bit column written by someone who called himself Masque. My letter complained about some of the stupid, nasty remarks that appeared there. These gay columns were filled with innuendo, such as "What well-known bartender had been out with what well-known queen?" I never approved of this kind of gay trivia. In my mind it does not contribute to the gay consciousness and is, frankly, demeaning and idiotic. But these columns were popular, and ran in almost all of the tabloids. Masque was succeeded at *TNT* by a gossip column entitled "A Study in Lavender," which began in January 1951. The column was written by several hands before being taken over by Mother Goose by 1952. Mother Goose also wrote "Fairy Tales Are Retold" for *The Rocket* as well as "Fairy Tales from Mother Goose" for *The Comet*. Bettina held forth in "Toronto Fairy-Go-Round," published in *Tab*, and was succeeded by Lady Bessborough's "The Gay Set," and so on[13].

Sir!, a popular New York men's magazine of the day, had published an article by Sara H. Carleton in its June 1950 issue entitled "The Truth About Homosexuals." It began: "Homosexuals can be cured — if they want to be. However, many prefer not to change their way of living." It went downhill from there. I was appalled, and was especially upset by the quoted remarks of Alfred A. Gross, executive secretary for the George W. Henry Foundation, who said, "'I have yet to meet a happy homosexual. They have a way of describing themselves as 'gay,' but the term is a misnomer. Those who are habitués of the bars frequented by others of their kind, are about the saddest people I've ever seen[14].'" This was a typical remark for the time, but I felt it could not go unchallenged. I sent a letter to the editor of *Sir!* expressing my outrage over the half truths and erroneous statements in the article. I said it was high time to publish an article detailing the case for homosexuality, written from a purely scientific viewpoint (using Hirschfeld, Ellis, Kinsey, et al.) and concluding with a consideration of the rights of the homosexual. Well, they were interested, and in the December 1950 issue of *Sir!* they published my article "I Am a Homosexual," under the pseudonym Leo Engle (the name of my maternal grandfather)[15]. It was about twenty-five hundred words and was published without many alterations. I was thrilled, and was even paid seventy-five dollars for it. It attracted quite a bit of attention, and several private letters written to Leo Engle were forwarded to me. I responded to these men, and corresponded with two of them for some time.

In early 1951 I had a fateful experience in the lobby of the Park Plaza Hotel. I met Theo L.J. Greenslade, who was at the time the editor of *True News Times*. We got into a conversation and I later wrote to him reminding him of our meeting, and went on to express my concern about the biased and prejudiced portrayal of homosexuals in *TNT*[16]. On 12 November 1951 I wrote a letter to *TNT*, suggesting that they might be interested in a series concerning homosexuality. They were, and they published my unsigned series "Aspects of Homosexuality" starting on 19 November 1951. This consisted of a full-page article each week and ran for seven weeks, through 31 December 1951[17]. I tried to write a balanced overview of particular aspects of homosexuality, with emphasis on homosexuality throughout history, the scientific, legal, and social aspects, and gay relationships. As far as I know, this was the first substantial series of articles published in Canada from a gay point of view. I was hoping that it would create a stir and that readers would write in to comment, or even to criticize. But the series barely caused a ripple and got very little in the way of publicity.

Jack and I were living at Oak Ridges during this time, and both of us were working full time. When I was doing the series for *TNT* I found it onerous meeting the damned deadline every week. I spent an awful lot of time at the typewriter and doing research in my library. I wanted to be careful not to make mistakes, as I didn't want anyone to check up on me. By the end of the series I was tired, and during 1952 I took a hiatus. I still typed a few letters that year, but not nearly as many as before. Jack and I spent much of our spare time that year building an addition onto our house.

From May 1951 the tabloid *Justice Weekly* published a number of my letters under the initials J.L.E., and some responses to the letters

TRUE NEWS TIMES

10c NATIONAL EDITION

Vol. 12, No. 45   Monday, November 19, 1951

Beginning New Series On Homosexuality

See Page 5

In a news story, dated Montreal, Nov. 9, 1951, in the *Globe and Mail*, Mr. St. Laurent was reported as having addressed McGill University and Macdonald College in a speech entitled "The Kind of Nation Canada Is." In it, he said, "... true unity does not involve the subjection of individual citizens to a common pattern or a common mould prescribed by an omnipotent state." Yet if this does not accurately describe the position of the homosexuals of Canada, I don't know what does. Further on, the Prime Minister says that every Canadian should emphasize to the various minorities that their rights would be safeguarded, and he adds, "I repeat my conviction that that is already true, but we all know it is not yet the conviction of many of our fellow citizens." One could assure the Prime Minister that he would have a hard time providing the validity of his conviction to the homosexuals of Canada. Here is one minority group whose rights are not only unprotected, but who have no rights to protect under present conditions.

From "More Tolerance Needed Toward Homos: Homosexuals 'Fall Guys' for Pressure Groups and Governments — Need to Be Properly Understood" (series, part seven), [by Jim Egan], *True News Times* (*TNT*), 31 December 1951, p. 5.

as well. *Justice Weekly* was another of the local tabloids with typical hysterical content, and I thought that they might publish some of my letters of protest. I believe they published almost every letter I sent to them. After I had written perhaps four or five letters, it occurred to me that perhaps they'd go for a series, much like I had published in *TNT*.

Philip H. Daniels was the proprietor, publisher, and editor of *Justice Weekly*. He was quite a character[18]. In 1953 the offices of *Justice Weekly* were located at Suite 206, Manning Chambers, 72 Queen Street West, which was above a block of ancient buildings filled with seedy pawn shops and second hand stores. The Municipal and Union House hotels were located at 67 and 71-73 Queen Street West, respectively. We used to refer to these hotels as "the Corners," as they were almost at the corner of Queen and Bay streets. The beverage rooms there were both equally grungy, and although of mixed male clientele were popular with working class gays, young hustlers, and the occasional drag queen. And, I must admit, I spent many a fascinating evening in them during my "salad days," as the Queen would say[19].

When I visited *Justice Weekly* one day in November 1953 I took with me a copy of what I saw as the first installment of a series entitled "Homosexual Concepts." I met Daniels and we had a talk. He was a genuine Cockney with a thick accent, and he immediately struck me as the embodiment of the stereotype of a sleazy editor of a Victorian, Grub Street scandal sheet. I introduced myself as the "J.L.E." of the letters that had been published in *Justice Weekly*. At that time I had a beard, which I have had for most of my adult life. Daniels looked up at me as I was explaining my idea for the "Homosexual Concepts" series. He thought about it for a minute and said, in his best Cockney, "Here, what's all this with you aping the male?" And I asked, "What do you mean?" "Well," he said, "you know, the beard. I didn't think fellows like you grew beards." Well, we got into quite a discussion. I pointed out to him there were truck drivers and loggers and construction workers and all kinds of people who were gay, and not all of them looked like bleached blonde hairdressers or interior decorators. Well, he was fascinated.

This was the only time I ever met Philip Daniels. I think he was neither friendly nor unfriendly towards me, and I certainly don't think he was necessarily liberal in his views of homosexuality. But he was interested in the idea of the series. He may have seen my

"Aspects of Homosexuality" series that had run in *True News Times* in 1951. I think Daniels agreed to publish "Homosexual Concepts" not because he necessarily supported the rights or aspirations of homosexuals but because my pro-gay writings were seen as a controversial novelty that might sell more copies of *Justice Weekly*. The idea that somebody would actually come out and defend the rights of gay people to live their own lives as they saw fit was unconventional. And, I must admit, I made a pitch to Daniels about how there were thousands of gay men and women in Toronto, and how they would probably be interested in these articles, and how this would likely increase his sales[20].

On 28 November 1953 *Justice Weekly* published an unsigned notice by me announcing that "Homosexual Concepts," a series of articles designed to "bring about a better understanding between hetero and homo," would commence the following week. The series ran in twelve parts, through 27 February 1954[21]. Its tone was similar to "Aspects of Homosexuality," but more ambitious. The 5 December article was an overview of the historical persecution of gays in England, in light of recent scandals involving well known figures such as Sir John Gielgud and Lord Montagu of Beaulieu[22]. Subsequent articles discussed The Mattachine Society, *ONE Magazine*, gay stereotypes, the Kinsey Report, gays and the media, gay bars, and other topics.

The series generated a few letters, but in terms of sales it was a failure. According to Daniels, the articles had no effect whatever on the paper's circulation. But Daniels treated me well. At the end of 1953, right after *Justice Weekly* published the first three articles in the series, I was surprised to receive a cheque in the mail for ten dollars for each of the three articles. I had no expectation of getting paid for the articles at all, and as I was then making thirty dollars a week this was a substantial amount of money to me.

Daniels and I were both disappointed with the reception of "Homosexual Concepts." I was annoyed that the so-called gay community didn't support the paper. I suppose some people bought the paper regularly just to keep track of gossip, arrests, police crackdowns, and so on. But many people thought of *Justice Weekly* as being just too lowbrow, and would never consider looking at it, even if it had good articles. I wasn't paid for any more articles in the series, but Daniels allowed me to continue writing.

I finished off "Homosexual Concepts" in February 1954, and

HOMOSEXUAL CONCEPTS
By "J. L. E."

Several weeks ago in one of these columns, I outlined a number of widely-held, but entirely erroneous misconceptions held by the average man-in-the-street regarding homosexuals and homosexuality. In succeeding columns I have tried to show the homosexual point of view; to try and correct these misconceptions, and in all these columns, from first to last, have endeavoured to bring about a better understanding between the normal and homosexual worlds. I do not for one moment think that any large number of my normal readers will agree with much that I have written. If, however, they have lost just a bit of prejudice and condemnation; if they are able to admit, now, that there is another side to the question and that a homosexual does have rights; if they have gained an insight into some aspect of homosexuality that might make it possible for them to have a better understanding of a son or brother; in short, if they are even prepared to admit now that the homosexual is not always the sex-mad degenerate they have been led to believe, the deep-dyed villain of the newspapers, then these columns have been worth-while.

The acceptance and integration that every thinking, responsible homosexual desires will come some day. There can be no possible doubt about that — it will come. But not overnight — or in a week or a month. Undoubtedly, it is going to take years of patient effort to overcome the prejudice, biased thinking and apathy that have surrounded the whole situation for so long. No tremendous change in public opinion has ever been effected in less than years, but before such change is remotely possible, of prime necessity is an enlightened public. Heretofore, little or no opportunity existed to present the "defence" — the public had heard only the "prosecution." If this column has brought understanding to even one reader, then the homosexuals are that much further along the road to emancipation.

From "Homosexual Concepts," by J.L.E., *Justice Weekly*, 27 February 1954, p. 13.

SUITE 206,   72 QUEEN ST. W.
TORONTO, ONTARIO, CANADA

• • •
EM. 8
—Telephone WAverly 5896—

Dec. 29, 1953,

Mr. James Egan,
P.O. Oak Ridges,
Ont.

Dear Mr. Egan,

         Enclosed cheque for ten dollars, will be the last one for material submitted. Lack of reader response does not justify any further expaniture for this type of material. Circulation has shown no noticable increase and letters have been received from only two readers, one of whom I feel you know pretty well.

         However, I am prepared to continue with the series but can continue to do so only on a non-cost basis. Let me know how you feel about the matter by return mail.

         Yours very truly,

P.H.D./A.G.

Correspondence from Philip Daniels concerning "Homosexual Concepts," 1953.

followed it with another, untitled series that continued for fifteen columns through 12 June 1954[23]. The themes of these columns were even more wide-ranging, from recent dismissals of homosexuals by the United States State Department, to additional examination of the Kinsey Report, to nature vs. nurture in the "cause" of homosexuality, and so on. These also generated letters from readers, but no increase in sales.

This was the end of the bulk of my contributions to *Justice Weekly*. In March 1955 Daniels did publish a brief I had sent to the Parliamentary Legislative Committee of the House of Commons concerning proposed amendments to Section 206 of the Canadian Criminal Code, regarding gross indecency[24]. Later he published another letter from me, as well as reprints of two articles originally published in *ONE Magazine*.

I am glad that I published these articles in *Justice Weekly*. The tabloid provided an outlet for my ideas, and at least some opportunity to introduce a gay-positive point of view into the Canadian press. I only wish there had been more response, but it was probably too early for that. And I think that Philip Daniels profited from the situation as well. Not in a monetary way, necessarily, but from new content for *Justice Weekly*. My columns filled pages of text, and were just the beginning of a flood of gay material that would be published in *Justice Weekly*. I suggested to Daniels that he write to some of the gay papers and offer them an exchange subscription. Apparently he did, and the papers agreed. Beginning with the issue of 6 February 1954, *Justice Weekly* regularly featured reprints of articles from *ONE Magazine*, and eventually other gay publications, including *The Ladder* [San Francisco], *The Mattachine Review* [San Francisco], *Arcadie* [Paris], *Der Kreis* [Zurich], *Vennen* [Copenhagen], and *Vriendschap* [Amsterdam]. Some of these articles were of high quality, and were written by leading gay writers and activists of the day such as James Barr, Donald Webster Cory, and Jim Kepner [writing as Lyn Pedersen][25].

I must say that when I was writing and researching my articles and letters I did feel sometimes that I was working in a vacuum. But I wasn't completely alone. My omnivorous reading habits continued unabated throughout this period, and I read all the gay classics I could find. I was particularly interested in the historical and philosophical aspects of homosexuality, and read works by Magnus Hirschfeld, Havelock Ellis, John Addington Symonds, Edward

Carpenter, and others. I read the classic works of Wilde, Proust, and Gide, and kept up with all the latest gay literature, from Vidal to James Barr's *Quatrefoil* [1950] to Fritz Peters's *Finistère* [1951], and others. And, I was able to contact gay activists elsewhere and in some cases engage in correspondence with them. For example, I was in contact with the Mattachine Society in Los Angeles from at least August 1953. My contact with them was limited, but I do remember corresponding with Hal Call[26]. I was more in contact with ONE, Incorporated, especially W. Dorr Legg [a.k.a. William Lambert][27], from about the same time. I subscribed to the publications of these organizations, and eventually was able to contribute articles to *ONE Magazine*.

During 1951 I conducted an extensive correspondence with Henry Gerber, who helped to organize the Society for Human Rights in Chicago in 1924, the first gay organization in the United States[28]. Between 16 January and 9 May I received at least eleven letters from him, but I regret that no carbon copies of my letters to him have survived. Gerber and I got along quite well on paper. When I was in contact with him he was living at the Soldier's Home in Washington, D.C. In May 1951 Gerber went on a trip to Europe for three months and that's the last I heard from him. I asked him to send me a copy of his early magazine, *Friendship and Freedom*, but he replied that he had destroyed all remaining copies long before. He did send me books and pamphlets, though, including André Gide's *Corydon* and *If It Die*.

In our correspondence Gerber and I disagreed on some things. For instance, Gerber was a social constructionist. He believed that all men are bisexual and that childhood experiences and societal influence determine whether a man becomes heterosexual or homosexual. I have always believed that homosexuality is a matter of genetics, that one is born absolutely destined to be a homosexual. I don't give a damn what kind of environment you grow up in, although I would readily admit that youthful environment may very well have a great deal to do with what *kind* of a homosexual you turn out to be. Environment may well play a role in whether a gay man is self-accepting, or a closet case. The way that gay men live may be a result of social constructionism, but the fact that they are gay in my opinion has nothing to do it. And what society would foster and encourage feelings of emotional, romantic, and sexual attraction between men, leading them to develop into homosexuals? No such

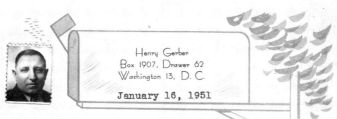

Henry Gerber
Box 1907, Drawer 62
Washington 13, D. C.

January 16, 1951

Dear Mr. Egan:

Saw your short notice in the Writers
Digest and thought I would write you
as we both seem to be admirers of
André Gide.

I received Corydon on Bebruary 13, 1950,
right after I saw it advertised in either
The Nation, the Saturday Review of Literature or Harpers. One of these publications
had a review of the book about this time.

Other books of Gide in my library are

The Journals, 3 volumes
The Immoralist
Oscar Wilde

On account of his outspoken homosexuality
Gide received a scant press here from the
hypocritical, stupid, uncivilized editors.
As you perhaps know, homosexuals are haunted
about and persecuted.

I am a retired army man living here at the
U.S. Soldiers home. Would like to hear
from you as I have plenty of leisure to
write and receive letters.

Sincerely yours

Henry Gerber

A letter from early American gay activist Henry Gerber, with a
photograph of Gerber attached, 1951.

Mattachine Society OFFICE OF THE COORDINATING COUNCIL

OAKLAND	LOS ANGELES
POST OFFICE BOX 851	POST OFFICE BOX 1925
OAKLAND 4, CALIFORNIA	MAIN POST OFFICE
	LOS ANGELES 53, CALIFORNIA

Los Angeles
August 20, 1953

James Egan
Oak Ridges,
Ontario, Canada

Dear Mr. Egan:

We have read with interest your letter of August 5, 1953
For your further information, we are enclosing some
literature published by the Mattachine Society.

Your efforts in correctly laying before the general public the whys and wherefores of the homosexual is needless
to say appreciated by the Society. Homosexuals need the
constant efforts on their behalf. It is of utmost importance that the Society make efforts toward the publication of material which accurately informs the general
public regarding homosexuality. We would be interested
in having you submit any paper which you think would be
of value along these lines.

We have referred your letter also to ONE Magazine, Inc.,
P.O. Box 5716, Los Angeles 55 , California for their information.

The Unitarian outlook on present day social problems is
indeed gratifying and the Society has been, since its
inception, in contact with various religious organizations
such as the Universalists and the Henry Foundation of the
Quakers. The Society believes that a sense of religious
values is a necessity for everyone in meeting his problems
of life, and even more so does this apply to the homosexual.

We hope to hear from you again very soon.

Sincerely,

MATTACHINE SOCIETY

KEN BURNS
Chairman
KB:mpr
Encl.

Correspondence from the Mattachine Society, Los Angeles, 1953.

society exists. Even in the golden age of Greece there were lots of men, I'm sure, who never, ever, engaged in homosexual behaviour, as opposed to expressing a homosexual orientation.

Beginning in mid-1954 I took another hiatus from gay activism. I sent few letters between then and early 1959, and my career as a gay activist was pretty much on hold. By 1954 I began to be affected by the fumes of the formaldehyde that was used in the preservation of the animal specimens I prepared. Thinking back to my days on the farm, I'm afraid I talked Jack into selling our property at Oak Ridges, which we did at a reasonable profit, and purchasing a farm in northwestern Ontario near a small town called Chesley. The farm was two hundred acres, including ninety-eight acres of workable land, seventy-five acres of hardwood bush, a twenty-five acre lake, and two acres of rough pasture. It had a nine-room solid brick house, an all-steel driving shed, and an all-steel barn. We paid nine thousand dollars for it, which seems hard to believe today. We had enough money to put a downpayment on the place and to purchase the necessary farm equipment to operate it. And we set about growing malting barley and raising pigs and turkeys. Eventually we made very good money on the pigs, and reasonable money on the malting barley, but we lost our shirts on the turkeys. After about two years, we realized that the harder we worked, the poorer we became. In order to make ends meet, I set up a crude embalming apparatus and started buying and embalming cats. We sold them to a company in the United States that was always looking for specimens. We sold as many as we could, and this helped to tide us over. Jack also took a job managing a hairstyling salon in the town of Chesley.

By mid-1956 Jack was very unhappy on the farm. He didn't care for it at all, and was particularly bothered by the financial uncertainty of farming. He was always saying, "Maybe we ought to sell. Maybe we ought to sell," but I was reluctant to do so. My mother was living with us at the time, and we had just about finished with the last batch of our turkeys.

We finally decided that we should get out of farming. I left Jack on the farm to look after the turkeys and I went down to the Niagara peninsula to a place called Beamsville. There I rented a store that had formerly been a pet shop, and that had a huge storage area behind. Jack and I had decided that we should get back into the biology business as a full-time occupation. Once people in Beamsville saw me moving things into the store, they came around and asked if we were

The farm, near Chesley, Ontario, 1956.

With Josephine Egan, at the farm, ca. 1955.

Jim in a field of barley, 1956.

going to re-open the pet shop, and we decided that eventually we would. In the meantime, I made arrangements with the Hamilton S.P.C.A. to buy the dead cats that they put down every day. I built a much more efficient embalming apparatus in the back storage area and began to embalm cats at high speed. This was quite a profitable pursuit in those days; at the time I didn't know of anyone else in Ontario who was doing this.

When the turkeys were ready for market I went back up to the farm. Some of our neighbours came over, and we loaded the turkeys into the big trucks and away they went. After we'd paid for the propane gas, for brooding the babies, and the starter and the grower and the finisher feed, we were six hundred dollars in the hole! That put the kibosh on the farm, as far as we were concerned. So we decided to both go down to Beamsville and to activate this biological supply business. I taught Jack the business, and from then on we worked as a team in preparing a variety of specimens — cats, especially, but also rabbits, frogs, and worms. We moved into the rickety little apartment above the store in Beamsville, and kept the farm as a weekend retreat. We drove to the farm every Friday night, stayed Saturday, and drove home on Sunday night.

One weekend we went up to the farm with the intention of figuring out how to renovate the huge old farmhouse, which had not been modernized. While Jack and I were standing outside talking, someone drove up. This man jumped out of the car and said, "I was wondering if you guys would be interested in selling the farm." Jack immediately said, "Yes, yes, yes, yes, yes," but I really didn't want to do it. So I thought I'd pull a fast one on this guy. I said, "Let me talk to my friend about this. Hang on here, and he and I will take a little walk." So I said to Jack, "All right, I know you want to sell the farm. Let's make him an offer. We'll offer to sell it for fourteen thousand dollars." At that time this was an absolutely ridiculous price to pay for a farm up there. But I realize now it was the lake and the woods and all the rest of it that attracted this man. He didn't want to farm the land at all. So, to our amazement, when we said fourteen thousand dollars he stuck out his hand and said, "It's a deal. I'll buy it!" I was a bit disappointed, but soon came to see that it was for the best. We sold the farm, and all the equipment, and settled into Beamsville to work very hard on developing our biology business.

In response to a number of requests from people in Beamsville, we decided to re-open the pet shop. We invested a couple thousand dollars in stock, and we sold canaries, budgies, and tropical fish. And Jack and I got into a very profitable sideline. There was a large number of European emigrants living in the area and they all grew monstrous gardens. They didn't want to buy seeds in little paper packages, the way you do today. So we bought seeds in bulk, at wholesale prices. We'd buy, say, ten pounds of turnip seeds. The store was fitted out with all these little drawers where the seeds were kept. People would come in and buy six ounces of turnip seed, or four ounces, or whatever, and the markup was absolutely incredible! Something like three or four hundred percent on the sale of seeds when you broke them down into small quantities. Anyway, the enterprise was eminently successful. We made a sign and called the store The Nature Shop, and we acquired the name The Nature Boys around Beamsville.

Eventually we started to look for another house to buy. Our real estate agent came charging in one day and said, "Have I got the house for you!" He took us up to show us this place, and I almost fainted when I looked at it. No one had lived in it for two or three years, and it was totally decrepit. The people who had lived there before must have been hillbillies because the house was surrounded by huge piles of food cans mixed with bottles and old clothes. What wasn't covered in garbage was covered in weeds that were four feet high. We beat our way through the place and looked at it. There was no furnace, no running water, no bathroom. The floors were all slanted. In addition to the house there was an old garage and ten acres of land on the Hamilton escarpment. Jack took one look at it and was absolutely ecstatic! He was convinced that this was the place we should buy. Well, the owners wanted ten thousand dollars, which was ludicrous. I'm sure Jack would have said, "O.K., we'll give you ten thousand dollars." But I told Jack, "Look, I don't want to buy this. There will be no end to renovating and repairing this place. So, let's offer thirty-five hundred dollars cash." Of course, I never thought they would accept. Well, I was defeated again and Jack and I ended up with this place. And I must admit that from the time we acquired that property everything turned up roses for us. We moved in there and had endless energy and enthusiasm, and we renovated the place. After about three years we had an absolutely gorgeous little home.

By 1959 we were sufficiently settled that I could return to spending more time on gay activism. I started to write letters again, and saw some of them published in *Look*, *Saturday Night*, the *Toronto*

Daily Star, and other magazines and newspapers. Jack and I were doing very well in our business and for the first time in our lives we were able to buy a new car, a Rambler. We decided to use the new car to go on a road trip and attend the fifth Midwinter Institute of ONE, Incorporated, in Los Angeles, from 30 January through 1 February 1959. Jack and I and another gay couple drove down to Los Angeles. The conference theme was "Mental Health and Homosexuality," and I found the seminars fascinating. We met W. Dorr Legg and Jim Kepner[29]. Kepner invited us to see his personal library and collection of gay memorabilia. We met Dr. Blanche Baker[30] and her husband William, who were one hundred percent gay positive. Blanche Baker was a great believer in psychodrama, and she was able to get us into a couple of sessions.

During one of the sessions Dorr Legg introduced me to Dr. Evelyn Hooker and told her that Jack and I had been together eleven years[31]. She was impressed by our long-term commitment and invited Jack and I out to her home, where she interviewed us for two or three hours on tape. She was charming, and I was glad to meet her. But, I read some of her works later on and I think she sometimes made very dubious statements. She believed that there was no such thing as a homosexual individual, but only individuals who engage in homosexual practices. And she contended that there is no such thing as a homosexual personality. I certainly don't agree with either of these statements.

It was also during 1959 that I had a wonderful exchange of letters with the Right Reverend Angus J. MacQueen, who was at that time the Moderator of the United Church of Canada[32]. MacQueen wrote a regular, inspirational column for the *Toronto Daily Star* called "The Church and You." One particular column was titled "Dare to Be 'Different,'" which was all about tolerance and understanding and acceptance of difference or non-conformity. You never read such a pile of hypocritical bullshit in your life! So I thought I'd play a trick on him. I wrote to MacQueen asking if his tolerance extended to supporting the loving, monogamous relationship of a devoted gay couple. His response advocated tolerance and understanding and liberality, except for those acts that are condemned in Scripture. We sent several letters back and forth, and I found it amusing that every letter the old boy sent to me was written in longhand. I think he didn't want his secretary to type it up and to see what he was writing. MacQueen did begin to moderate his tone a bit and was not quite so

The homosexual "marriage" certainly requires work if it is to succeed. But it is questionable if one ever achieves much in this world without willingness to work and sacrifice when necessary. And in few cases does this hold more true than in that of two homosexuals who wish to spend their lives together. As a speaker remarked at last year's Mid-Winter Institute while discussing this subject, "Fifty-fifty is not enough, each must contribute at least 60% to the effort." The unwillingness to do so accounts for a good many of the break-ups. There are, of course, other causes as well: those "other pastures" that look so deceptively green, the foolish, petty jealousies and — so often — the incompatibility that exists in every room in the place other than the bed-room. The successful homosexual relationship is composed of many elements: love, trust, mutual respect, co-operation and, above all the determination on the part of both partners to remain together in spite of what family, friends or anyone else thinks, says or does.

Apart from these requirements that must be present, there is still another that is a prerequisite not only to the successful relationship, but which is equally essential to the happiness of the single homosexual. I refer to the ability to accept oneself as a homosexual — completely without reservation or guilt. That many cannot do so is, I firmly believe, the cause of so much of the misery and unhappiness that besets their lives and so often sets them upon the downward path that leads to the psychiatrist's couch.

From "Homosexual Marriage ... Fact or Fancy?," by Jim Egan, *ONE Magazine,* December 1959, p. 7.

vituperative towards the end of our correspondence. He even asked that I recommend books or articles that he might read to gain a better understanding of the "problem" of homosexuality. So I bundled up several books, one of which I recall was Cory's *The Homosexual in America*, as well as copies of *ONE Magazine*, and mailed them off to him. MacQueen mailed them back four months later, saying that the pressure of church business was such that he didn't think he had time to read all of them, but he thanked me for my interest.

My experience with Reverend MacQueen was similar to one I'd had earlier with Fulton Sheen. Sheen was an American Roman Catholic bishop who was the host of an enormously popular religious television program during the 1950s[33]. The set was made up to look like his study. When the program opened the bishop swished onto the set in his ecclesiastical drag, with the crucifix swinging, and threw his arms open to say, "God bless you all." The program was non-denominational and consisted mostly of sanctimonious platitudes. In one of his programs Sheen said that the role of the true Christian was to be accepting and understanding of people who were different, and that it was a very serious sin for a Christian to point the finger of criticism and scorn at others because they didn't share his beliefs. He went on and on and on. I thought, "Well, isn't that interesting." So I sat myself down and wrote him a letter. I wrote that I was part of a gay couple who'd been together for a number of years, were very much in love, and had a monogamous relationship. We did have a problem, though, with the conflict we felt between our relationship and the teachings of the Roman Catholic Church. Believe me, the last part was a pure figment of the imagination! I asked Bishop Sheen if he could offer us some word of comfort. The response I received was signed, I presume, by one of his secretaries. It was one of the most outrageous responses imaginable, considering the letter I had sent. This idiot said that we were living in a state of sin, we were doomed to eternal damnation, and we were doubling the seriousness of the sin — the culpability — by trying to justify it. He ordered us to separate at once and never see each other again. I recall I was so infuriated by this letter that I crumpled it up into a ball and threw it in the fireplace. And then I sat down and wrote a blistering letter in reply, pointing out that if my original letter had been legitimate the response might well have initiated two suicides. So much for compassion and understanding of those who are different.

The house at Beamsville, Ontario, 1960.

The Nature Boys, ca. 1960.

Chapter Five: Gay Personalities of Old Toronto

As an early gay activist in Toronto, I knew dozens of gay and bisexual men. Here are my random memories of a few of the personalities and characters who were active in the gay community then.

George Hislop

Jack and I have known George Hislop from when he was considered a chicken in the gay world! We knew him even before he met Ralph Anderson, who was George's partner before he met Ronnie Shearer. But apart from meeting him at the occasional party or running into him downtown and listening to the latest tale of woe about the latest boyfriend, we were not really very close to George.

As far as I can remember, George didn't have tendencies towards gay activism back in the 1950s. His interest in gay liberation really didn't take off until the 1960s. In about 1965 or 1966, after Jack and I had moved to the West Coast, George sent me a letter saying that he felt the time was ripe to start a gay organization in Toronto. In reply I sent George a five-inch reel to reel tape with advice about what I would do if I were starting up a gay group there[1]. Of course, George's enthusiasm and hard work eventually led to the formation of the Community Homophile Association of Toronto (CHAT) in December 1970[2].

Peter Marshall

We knew Peter to see him, but that was all. Once in a while Jack and I would be sitting in the Chez Paree Restaurant [located at 220 Bloor Street West] and Peter would come in with his entourage of chickens and sweep by with the bleached blonde hair. You know, your typical wealthy older queen.

Peter was a flamboyant character who was famous for holding parties up in Rosedale. We heard all about them and knew people who had been to them. But I don't think that Jack and I, in those days, would have been really into that lifestyle. We didn't move in those circles. As I'm sure is the case today, gay life in Toronto in the 1950s and 1960s was on a series of levels, with your opera queens and the highly educated university types at the top, and the ribbon clerks at Simpson's at the bottom. While there may have been a certain amount of overlap, we didn't associate with anybody except from what we might refer to as the "lower orders." And I say that in the kindliest way, because we were part of it.

The Chez Paree Restaurant, Toronto, ca. 1956. Photo by Jones and Morris.

Jimmy Roulston

Jimmy Roulston used to play either the piano or one of those electric organs at the Chez Paree. Most outrageous! Back in the 1950s, in the evening the Chez Paree was patronized mainly by gay men. It was a very nice restaurant. I'll always remember one night in particular. Jimmy sat with his piano on a bit of a dais, above the floor, and people would get up and ask him to play a particular number. On this evening, a tall, elegant, Clifton Webb type went up. Jimmy leaned down and this guy whispered, "Will you play so and so." And he turned around to go back to his table just as Jimmy spoke into the microphone and said, "I've just had a request from my dear sister so-and-so to play this number." This poor man looked so embarrassed I thought he'd drop dead in his tracks! Jimmy was that sort of flamboyant, in-your-face type.

Jimmy was one of those people like a ship that passes in the night. Jack and I saw him from time to time, we knew who he was, but I'm not sure that I ever even spoke to him. I do remember walking along Bloor Street once in the summertime, though. Jimmy was just ahead of me, and there was quite a crowd of people all around us. Just as we got to Bay Street, the light turned red. And Jimmy looked around at all these people and said, "My God. It never fails! Every time I get to a street corner the light turns red!" These people were wondering what *this* was all about. Jimmy was just a fun person[3].

Frances and Geraldine

Two characters stand out in my memories of the Corners. It is hard to say how old they were when I knew them. I don't know if I ever knew their real names, although everyone called them Frances and Geraldine. Frances was a black guy who weighed two hundred pounds at the absolute minimum and was always plastered with makeup, including green eye shadow and lipstick. He dressed in a unisex way so that it was difficult to tell whether you were looking at a man or a woman. Geraldine was the very mirror opposite. He was also about two hundred pounds but with porcelain features and makeup galore. The two of them were great sisters. They were hustlers. They'd come to the Corners in the evening to drink beer and look for clients. I don't know that they made many pickups at the Corners, but they would cruise the streets and some horny heterosexual would pick them up. They'd say that it was the wrong time of the month, but they could give him a good blow job! Frances and Geraldine could pass, especially back then, because the average straight man meeting them really wouldn't question that they were women. I was great friends with both of them.

I remember one night there at the Corners. The two of them were sitting at a table, as usual, together, dishing up a storm about something. Four or five really rough looking numbers came in and took seats in the middle of the room, and kept glaring over at Frances and Geraldine. And they knew they were being looked at. The more the guys looked at them, the more flamboyant they became. So, finally, Frances got up to go to the washroom, and two seconds later one of these guys from the table got up and followed him. And in about half a minute you never heard such screams and shrieks coming out of the washroom! Frances was whaling the shit out of this tough guy. The bartender jumped over the bar and went in with a sawed off pool cue and dragged this straight one out and threw him out the front door. The gay ones were always protected down there, but in this particular instance Frances handled the situation very well.

Miss Jeffries

There was a wonderful character who used to frequent the Corners. I don't know why, but nobody ever sat with him. Nobody ever talked to him. Everybody referred to him as Miss Jeffries. He was this absolutely fragile little creature. I don't suppose he weighed more than ninety pounds. He was sort of pretty, in a refined kind of way, and always wore these vinyl jackets. Quite stylish, but very aloof.

The beverage rooms at the Corners were mixed, you know. They weren't by any means exclusively gay. Everyone sat around in a mixed group, and for the most part minded their own business. The straight ones that came in were usually older men, rough workmen types. They sat down and drank their beer. Miss Jeffries used to come in, and like several others we knew would proceed with a ritual after he sat down. All this fussy business about arranging the change in one pile, and the cigarette lighter, and the keys, and all the time brushing back the hair and fluttering up the collar.

One evening a big, elderly, rough workman was sitting kitty-corner from Miss Jeffries, and was absolutely open-mouthed with amazement. He couldn't figure out what *it* was. Miss Jeffries didn't do anything for awhile, but was well aware that he was being stared at. Finally he turned around and looked at this old guy and said, "Well, do you want to fuck or fight?" The man was just thunderstruck! He gulped his beer down, got up, and fled.

The Municipal Hotel, Toronto, part of the Corners, ca. 1952.
Photo by Jones and Morris.

The beverage room, Municipal Hotel, Toronto, ca. 1952.
Photo by Jones and Morris.

Madame Butterfly

There was a man who used to hang around the tavern at the Savarin Hotel who was known as Madame Butterfly. He had been an opera singer in his youth but had wrecked his voice. He had this husky, husky voice and every sentence was preceded by the hand on the chest — that gesture. He was a panic. There were quite a few characters like him around. But, apart from running into them in the pub, I never socialized with any of them at all. They were just casual acquaintances.

Fred "Scotty" Wilson and Art Truman

Jack and I knew Scotty for many years, although when we knew him he was no longer called Scotty but was known as Tiny. He was a truly hilarious gay man. Tiny was a born entertainer, and had gained some fame as a comedian in overseas shows for the Allied troops during World War Two.

When we knew Tiny he must have weighed two hundred seventy-five pounds, with chins on the chins on the chins. The moment he walked into a room he simply took over. He had a charismatic aura about him. Everybody just sat there, fascinated. And Tiny would never stop. He would hold forth — he was on, as the saying goes, from the time he walked in and would skip from one thing to the next. He sounded very Churchillian when he spoke, quite the sonorous tones. But in the blink of an eye he could grab up a throw from a chesterfield and put it around his shoulders, place a lampshade on his head, and be transformed into Queen Victoria inspecting the plumbing at Buckingham Palace. He kept everyone in fits.

When Tiny was in World War One he met another young guy about his own age, Art Truman. Those two were together for more than forty years, right up until Tiny's death in 1959. As Tiny and Art grew older I think they were absolutely devoted to each other, but in the latter years were not quite what you would call lovers, just absolutely devoted friends. They used to address each other as Miss Wilson and Miss Truman. Art used to dance attendance on Tiny all the time. He used to fuss over him like a little mother hen with baby chicks. It was a delight to see the two of them together. But when Tiny died there was not a word in the death notice about poor little Art[4]. After Tiny died I think Art only lived for maybe a year, and then he followed him.

Alex Bakalis

I used to see Alex Bakalis fairly often at the Corners. He was about forty years old and worked as a clothing salesman. We became pretty good friends, on a purely Platonic level. One night early in May 1960 Alex and I were sitting in the tavern of the Union House Hotel when this young guy came in. His name was Joseph Normandin and he was a handsome fellow, about twenty years old. But other gay men had mentioned to me that he was really unbalanced and unstable. He was strictly a hustler, not a young gay man who was just looking for sex.

That night Alex happened to glance over and say, "Oh, there's Joseph. I'm off." I said, "Gee, Alex, you'd better watch out. That kid has a dreadful reputation." Alex replied, "Oh, I can handle him. I've had him half a dozen times." Well, they left together and that's the night that Alex was murdered.

The local papers covered the murder and related how Alex took Normandin back to his apartment on Farnham Avenue. They had a falling out, and Normandin stabbed Alex numerous times, first in the back with a steak knife, then with a butcher knife. Normandin fled the apartment with Alex's wallet but later surrendered to a policeman.

Alex's murder became quite the cause célèbre for me because I had seen them go off together. I was also keenly interested to see how the case would be handled, both in court and in the newspapers. I attended the preliminary hearing, during which Normandin's lawyer tried to put forward the bullshit argument that his client, a fine, upstanding, blue-eyed, Canadian boy, had been assaulted by a vicious pervert.

After the hearing I waited in the corridor outside to talk to Normandin's lawyer. I told him that Alex was a friend of mine and I had been in the hotel the night that Alex went over and picked this kid up, as he had done several times before. I didn't intend to sit by and allow him to use this defence to get this boy off scot-free. I told him that if he persisted in it I'd go to the Attorney General's office and declare myself a friend of the court. Then I'd testify that I knew that Normandin was a professional hustler in Toronto and that he was certainly not an innocent youth. I'm not much in favour of vindictive vengeance because I don't think that serves much of a purpose, but I didn't want to see Alex defamed in this way.

The lawyer's reaction was quite amusing. He listened to what I had to say and said, "Well, I don't think you're really serious because you know that if you got on the witness stand and testified like that everybody would know what you are." And I said, "Well, it doesn't bother me. That's the point. I don't care whether everybody knows what I am." When the trial came up Normandin's lawyer didn't try that tactic at all. Normandin pleaded guilty to a charge of manslaughter, reduced from murder. The defence lawyer acknowledged that Normandin was a disturbed young man, and it came out that he had worked as a hustler for five years. In the end, Normandin was sentenced to life imprisonment[5].

Few minority groups have ever had to contend with the degree of discrimination or the denial of civil right to which the homosexual is subject. While recent legislation has made it virtually impossible for the bigoted to discriminate against any minority in matters relating to housing, jobs or public accommodation, this protection, unfortunately, does not extend to the homosexual and he remains the relatively helpless victim of a society which seems determined not to lose their sole remaining scapegoat.

Under present federal legislation, the homosexual, if he wishes to remain within the law, is condemned to a lifetime of enforced celibacy — in spite of our celebrated Canadian Bill of Rights which prohibits any law that would "impose or authorize the imposition of cruel and unusual treatment or punishment." The alternative to celibacy is a possible life term in prison as a criminal sexual psychopath upon conviction of a single offence. These laws are all the more unjust in that in so far as consenting adults, in private, are concerned the activity outlawed is in no slightest way detrimental to the welfare of society nor could it be described as "criminal" by even the most violent distortions of logic.

Sexual acts, between consenting adults, in private — regardless of the sex of the participants — are strictly matters of private morality and neither the law nor society can justify their insolent intrusion into this sphere of human behavior.

From "Civil Liberties and the Homosexual," by James Egan, *Toronto Daily Star*, 23 October 1963, p. 7.

Chapter Six: Explorations of Gay Male Community in Toronto in the Early 1960s

As letters and articles were published under my own name, I eventually became recognized as a gay activist in the small town of Beamsville. I must say that even back then there was never any antagonism shown towards Jack or myself. We never had any homophobic slurs thrown at us, or anything like that. But, as time went by, Jack became increasingly uncomfortable with our situation there. He didn't like the publicity. In the fall of 1963 Jack suggested that we move back to Toronto. I agreed. We sold the place near Beamsville and moved to Toronto, where we took an apartment at 1052A Bloor Street West, above the Bloor Supermarket.

One day, shortly after our move back to Toronto, I got a telephone call from Sidney Katz, who was an associate editor at *Maclean's*[1]. He had been commissioned by the magazine to do an article on the gay community of Toronto. Katz said he'd read some of the pieces I'd written. He wanted to do the article but said that he knew almost nothing about homosexuality. He wondered if I would be willing to cooperate with him, not in helping to write the article but in talking to him about homosexuality and gay life. I was pleased to help, and invited him up to our apartment. One of the bedrooms there had been converted into a library-study, and the walls were lined with bookcases. I had dozens of books dealing with homosexuality, some of them quite old and rare. I regret that I've lost, disposed of, or sold a lot of them since then. Katz came up and he and I talked for I don't know how long, and I loaded him down with all kinds of books, papers, and clippings to read.

Katz later came back to the apartment for two or three visits and we talked about aspects of the gay life that he had no knowledge of at all. At that time police were criticising certain local clubs as being "hangouts for male and female homosexuals[2]." Katz asked me about these places and I invited him to do a round of the bars on a Saturday night. He agreed.

We started off down at the Corners. We went down there at about eight-thirty at night, when they were at their mildest, because frankly I didn't want him to see them at eleven, when they were at their height. We hit the beverage rooms at the Municipal and the Union House hotels.

We left the Corners and walked north on Bay Street, heading for

One evening, in the company of a homosexual guide [Egan], I visited two of Toronto's lowest gay taverns. One tavern consisted of a long, shabby, depressing room. Most of the men were "masculine-type" homosexuals, dressed in sloppy work clothes. Other guests — most of these over forty — were conspicuous by their neat and conventional attire. Entering and leaving the tavern and table-hopping were a number of youths — male prostitutes soliciting the other men....

Tourists who come to the gay bars to stare are discouraged in different ways. In one bar, the regulars will point and stare at the offending "straight" people, whisper among themselves and then burst out laughing. After this routine is repeated a few times, the tourists retreat in confusion and dismay. One night, a party of gay people found themselves next to a table of giggling, finger-pointing heterosexuals. One of the homosexuals leaped up and, in a loud, shrill female voice, said, "I must now go, my dears. Your poor mother is exhausted after washing, ironing and cooking all day."

From "The Homosexual Next Door," by Sidney Katz, *Maclean's*, 22 February 1964, p. 29.

the beverage room at the Ford Hotel [at 595 Bay], which was at the corner of Bay and Dundas streets across from the bus terminal. In those days Bay was a very dark and gloomy street at night. There was absolutely nothing doing. As we were walking north I suddenly saw heading south, obviously to the Corners, a gay character that I knew. His name was Fred. I never did know his last name. He was about fifty-five years old, a little on the overweight side but not too bad. Under ordinary circumstances he was a perfectly normal appearing man. But when he started to camp it up, there was nobody who could hold a candle to Fred. He was absolutely outrageous, and truly hilarious.

Fred was a painter, and a very successful one. He used to paint street scenes, with light reflecting on rainy streets populated by stick-like figures and tall apartment buildings. Fred used to churn out these paintings in an endless production line. He could never produce them fast enough. There were galleries all around Toronto buying them up from him. Fred spent every nickel that he made on street kids. He liked the sixteen- or seventeen-year-olds, and there were lots of them around in Toronto in those days if you knew where to look.

So Sidney Katz and I were walking north and we were talking about what he just saw at the Corners and I saw Fred approaching from about a block away. I recognized him and thought, Oh, my God, of all the people I'd want us to run into the last would be Fred. When Fred finally recognized me he paused and said [in a lispy voice], "Hi, Jim. How are you tonight?," and he really went into his little act. And I said, "Hello, Fred. How are things going? Off to the Corners?" "Oh, yes." And then he looked like a coy girl, and got himself all wrapped around himself, and said "And who is your most *attractive* gentleman friend?" I nearly *shit*, to tell you the truth. Sidney was looking at him absolutely open-mouthed. So I said, "This is Sid, a friend of mine. This is Fred. We've got to get going, Fred. We'll see you later." And so we took off. I often wonder whatever happened to Fred.

We arrived at the Ford Hotel and just had a beer there. It had a mixed gay-straight beverage room. There wasn't very much doing. From there we went to the Red Lion, at the Westbury Hotel [at 475 Yonge Street]. It was a very popular hangout at that time and had a huge beverage room. I guess it was getting on to ten-thirty when we got there, and it was packed. There were probably two hundred fellows in that place. We sat down at a corner table for two and

... the homosexual, in growing numbers, is becoming bolder in his campaign to be accepted as a member of society in good standing. Homosexuals are demanding the right to live their private lives in their own way without censure or penalty. At present, the legal bar to equality is Section 149 of the Criminal Code, which states that "every one who commits an act of gross indecency with another person is guilty of an indictable offense and is liable to imprisonment for five years." Sexual union between two members of the same sex is interpreted as "gross indecency," making a practising homosexual, *ipso facto*, a criminal.... Verne Baldwin [Jim Egan]..., a highly educated forty-three-year-old homosexual, speaks for the newly militant homosexual when he says, "As the first step towards justice, Section 149 should be abolished. It's a vicious law. Nobody is harmed by two consenting adults who perform, in private, what comes naturally to them. Jews, Negroes and other minorities are now protected by anti-discrimination legislation. We homosexuals are society's remaining scapegoats."

From "The Homosexual Next Door," by Sidney Katz, *Maclean's*, 22 February 1964, p. 10.

ordered a beer. Katz was looking around. He was very discreet. Sidney never resembled a tourist. Eventually he leaned over to me and asked, "How many of the fellows in here do you suppose are gay?" I said, "Well, I know a great many of them by sight and there are some I don't know, but I imagine that ninety-five percent are." Katz replied, "Well, what is that idiot chief of police talking about? The way he describes a gay beverage room as some sort of den of iniquity, with degenerate looking people. I don't see any fellow in here that I wouldn't be proud to call my son as far as personal appearance is concerned." So he certainly got his eyes opened on that.

I'm not sure where I took him from there. There were a couple of other places. Eventually, late that night, we ended up way over on College Street in some little restaurant that must have been open all night.

Sidney Katz's "The Homosexual Next Door: A Sober Appraisal of a New Social Phenomenon" was published as a two-part series in *Maclean's* magazine during February-March 1964[3]. These are considered to be the first full-scale articles published in a mainstream Canadian publication to take a generally positive view of homosexuality. I have talked to people who weren't overly impressed by them, claiming that they were not sufficiently supportive of gays. I thought they were fair and objective. Considering that they were written by someone like Katz, who was not gay, the articles were refreshingly non-judgmental for the time, and very informative. In the first part, "The Homosexual Next Door," he quoted me extensively under the pseudonym Verne Baldwin (Jack was "George Galbraith"). In the second part Katz went after opinions from psychiatrists at the Forensic Clinic, religious leaders, and other "authorities." I had no further contact with Sidney at all. I feel I was somewhat remiss in not writing to him and thanking him for writing a good piece.

I was afraid that *Maclean's* would be swamped with letters of protest about these articles. I had visions of the pulpits being emptied while all the clergymen rushed to their typewriters to dash off letters of bitter protest. So I sat down and wrote four or five relatively brief letters praising *Maclean's* for publishing the articles, and signed them all with false names. Well, my fears were unfounded. *Maclean's* published three letters, all of which were supportive[4].

In connection with all of this I should mention that I had a friend in Toronto by the name of Saul. He worked as a despatcher for a large ready-mix cement company and was one of my favorite people. One day I got a telephone call from him, and he asked me if I was free in a day or two to have lunch with him. I said sure. He said there was someone he'd be bringing along who wanted to meet me. I said fine, I'd be glad to meet him.

We met at the Chez Paree. I came into the restaurant and glanced around. There was Saul sitting at a table with this very tall, distinguished, gray-haired gentleman with a hand-polished leather face. He was just oozing money, position, and power, and was a very charming man. Certainly you would never jump to the conclusion he was gay just by meeting him. The man looked like a lawyer, perhaps, or a wealthy stockbroker or real estate man. Saul introduced me on a first name basis only, and I don't remember the man's name. He ordered a delightful light lunch for the three of us.

Afterwards, we lit cigarettes and were sitting there talking for awhile, and he said, "Well, I've asked Saul to bring us together because I have something very serious I want to talk about with you. A group of us were discussing the matter the other night, and we understand that you are about to collaborate with Sidney Katz on publishing an article about the gay community in Toronto." I said that was correct. He continued, "Well, we think it's very unwise. My friends and I are very concerned about this and we think you should not do it. You should change your mind and inform Katz that you will not cooperate with him." I was thunderstruck, and replied, "Why on Earth would you feel concerned about this? As far as I'm concerned, this is the opportunity of a lifetime: to have an article published in a national magazine like *Maclean's* in which I will have some influence to ensure its accuracy." Well, he said, "you've been writing a lot of stuff in the papers lately and I understand you're going on Pierre Berton's show." I said, "Yes[5]." He replied, "The thing is, if you keep on publicizing this the way you are, it won't be possible for any gay man to be safe. People will begin to get suspicious and gay men will be recognized as living a gay life. Now, one can live a quiet, unobtrusive life, and nobody suspects that the forty-five or fifty-year-old man who is unmarried and lives in a bachelor apartment, or maybe even shares an apartment with another man, may be gay. But if you keep this up, they're going to know about it." And I said, "Well, to tell you the truth, that's exactly my purpose. Frankly, there's nothing I would like better than for every homosexual in Toronto to be exposed overnight as a homosexual, simultaneously, and the problem would be solved. There is absolutely nothing society could do about it." Well, he was quite horrified by this and although he was very polite and reasonable, we discussed it at great length. I finally ended up saying that I wouldn't even dream of backing off on this. So Sidney Katz's articles were written with some assistance from me, and I was pleased with the result.

It was at about this time that my relationship with Jack came under severe pressure. We had been back in Toronto for a few months when Jack announced that either I give up gay activism or our relationship was at an end. I was becoming so involved in this that our telephone was ringing all the time. I was involved in battles with the local newspapers, particularly the *Telegram*. I had one hell of a row with them. We were phoning backwards and forwards because they were trying to ignore a response that I had written to a series of three terrible articles they had published on the "shadow world" of the homosexual, entitled "Society and the Homosexual," written by "a senior *Telegram* staff reporter" [Ron Poulton][6]. Sidney Katz and Pierre Berton had phoned a number of times. I was also getting calls from complete strangers who were looking for a crisis line.

By that time Jack and I had been together for more than fifteen years and he was totally fed up with gay activism. In those days Jack had a straightforward view of gay life. He thought that if you're gay, you meet someone and settle down with them. Then as a couple you live a quiet, unobtrusive life. Don't interfere with anyone, and they won't interfere with you. I'm afraid Jack felt that most gay men who ran afoul of the law were in their predicament because of their own foolishness. But I didn't see it quite that way at all. We had a long talk one night and Jack said that he had not become involved in a relationship to become a gay activist. He didn't like the notoriety associated with this sort of activism, and couldn't avoid it unless I gave up my public involvement in gay issues. I, on the other hand, had made up my mind that I was going to stick to it. This was very important to me. I couldn't just walk away from it and tried to convince Jack to accept the fact, but no, it wouldn't do. I foolishly said, "All right, if that's the way it's going to be, so be it." So we separated. We split the bank account down the centre and I took half and he took half. At that time I was working in a bookstore on Bloor Street, trying to get it organized. I quit this job and set up another business preserving biological specimens, primarily white rats and cats. I rented a workroom in the Spadina-College district and lived in a one-room apartment above. Jack kept living in our old apartment.

After Jack and I split up, I began to spend a fair amount of time during the evenings at the Music Room, one of Toronto's first gay clubs [located upstairs at 575 Yonge Street][7]. The Music Room was owned by Rick Kerr, a gay man, and Sara Ellen Dunlop, a lesbian. The club didn't have a liquor licence so it attracted people as young as sixteen and seventeen. People went there to have coffee and conversation and to dance. Drag shows were also held there. Murray Burbidge [a.k.a. Toni Seven] was one of the leading drag queens in Toronto at the time, and he used to perform often. I would say he was semi-professional. Murray made all his own costumes, and was excellent.

When I went to the Music Room I would often chat with Rick Kerr. Rick was usually on the door, both to welcome people coming into the club and to make sure that the wrong type didn't get in. Rick was a relatively small guy, maybe five foot eight and about one hundred forty-five pounds, but he could be a scrapper if he had to be. I remember a guy who came in there one night and started to create trouble. Rick dragged him over to the door and started to beat him up. Sara was in a panic and yelled, "Stop it! You're going to kill him." Rick was right on the point of throwing the guy down the stairs.

Some of the kids who went to the Music Room were having real trouble coming to terms with their sexual orientation. They would try to engage Rick in conversation, and he'd bring them over to the table where I was sitting and ask me to talk to them. Often some guy would wander into the club in a panic after he'd finally realized he was gay, or he had known for some time and he just wanted to talk about it. Gay people today have no idea what it was like being gay in those days. Homosexuality was not discussed openly in polite society. There were no positive gay role models. Many young gays felt there was absolutely no one to turn to or to talk to. In Toronto, there were no support groups of any kind. So Rick directed a few of these people to me and we had interesting conversations.

I remember one young fellow in particular who had just arrived in Toronto from some place in the country, a farming area. He was one of the nicest boys I'd ever met, although nothing happened between us. He was an extremely attractive, fresh-faced farm boy who was really in a bad mental space. We sat and talked for awhile

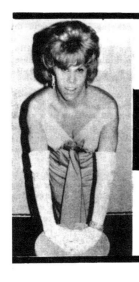

Kick up your heels and have a gay swinging time. Dining and dancing until 4.30 a.m. - on the week-end until 2. a.m. throughout the week.

MUSIC ROOM

MELODY ROOM

Toronto's original after-hours gay clubs. Offering you a complete range of facilities from the quiet intimacy of our TV lounge to lively floorshows featuring Toronto's finest Female Impersonators.

The steep, barren staircase is an unlikely entrance to a place so warm and vital. Once the red and gold door is passed, the world of Yonge Street swiftly fades from memory. Rich wine drapes with the flocked wallpaper, plush red wall-seats and the textured white ceiling all combine to relax the visitor into an easy mood of gaiety....

Sociable mixing is easy at the Music Room; it is small and bright enough for a friendly smile to be visible across the room. The wall-seats make it possible to sit strategically near someone, while working up the courage to propose a dance, without actually walking up to the table. Those who choose to devote themselves to each other without unwelcome interruption, may do so in the alcove corner just off the stage.

From "Music Room Private Members Club," by Peter Alann, *Two*, no. 3 (1964), p. 23.

and eventually he told me that he had been aware of his feelings for other boys, and his entire lack of feeling for girls, for as long as he could remember. He didn't hate women, but they held no sexual attraction for him at all. His father had died and he'd convinced his mother that she should sell the farm, because he really wasn't into farming. So she sold the farm and moved to town, where she was quite comfortable. He saw this as his big break to go to Toronto, where he began to investigate the gay world. He was absolutely horrified by what he found. I asked him what had upset him about it. "Well," he said, "I don't want to become like them." He pointed out to the dance floor, which was occupied by twelve or fifteen seventeen- or eighteen-year-old shrieking, screaming queens who were carrying on in the most outrageous fashion. They were absolutely fantastic dancers, every one of them, and were having a great time, but were screaming and shrieking and camping it up and carrying on. I told him there was no reason in the world he must turn into one of those types. In my opinion, they were that way through choice. They had chosen that lifestyle, and he must choose his. They find acceptance among other young guys who behave like themselves, and that's fine. But just because you're gay doesn't mean you have to act like that. The young guy seemed relieved. This is just the sort of identity crisis that many young gay men face when they first become aware of their sexual orientation, and I hope that in my conversations at the Music Room I was able to allay some fears concerning the gay life.

During those early days at the Music Room, sometimes on a Thursday night the music would stop at around ten and everyone would sit around and talk about gay life in Toronto. There would sometimes be fifty or sixty people at these informal discussions. At that time I was really interested in the idea of helping to establish some sort of formal gay organization in Toronto. I had been in touch with ONE, Incorporated, quite a bit, and I had asked Dorr Legg if they would agree to the formation of a Toronto branch of ONE. Dorr was quite enthusiastic and asked me to see what I could do. Well, whatever talents I may have, organization is not one of them. I didn't have a clue as to how to go about organizing a group like that. I really wanted someone else to act as organizer, and I would certainly have helped. The idea was eventually abandoned as I found that not many others were interested in it at all.

Sometimes outsiders would come to talk at these discussions at the Music Room. I remember on one occasion three or four psychiatrists from the Forensic Clinic came and they had a lot to say. One psychiatrist was holding forth and one of the boys in the audience asked this doctor point blank, "Do you think all gay men are sick?" The doctor hedged about it a bit and said, "I think all gay men are by definition neurotic and in one sense of the word, yes, *sick*, and require treatment." And so the kid asked, "Why do you think we're all sick?" The doctor replied, "Because of your inability to engage in normal sexual intercourse with a woman." Then the kid asked, "Well, why do you think we do not engage in normal sexual intercourse?" The doctor said, "Because the homosexual male is afraid to make the effort for fear he fails. He fears failure in the act and doesn't try." So the kid thought about that and sat down and nobody else said anything. So I said, "Now, wait a minute. How could you possibly fear failure of an act you have not the slightest desire to commit? If I were sitting here drooling over girls and wishing I could go to bed with them but was afraid to make the effort, yea. But what if you don't have the faintest desire in the world to go to bed with a woman and you have no desire to succeed at all? How could I be afraid of failure?" The doctor didn't have much of an answer for this. I think he replied that I had succeeded in convincing myself that I really wasn't interested. But that was just the sheerest sophistry, as far as I was concerned[8].

Shortly after Sidney Katz's articles appeared in *Maclean's* I received a telephone call from a man who introduced himself as Dr. William Hogg, a psychiatrist with the Forensic Clinic in Toronto. He had read the articles and had contacted Sidney Katz, and Katz gave him my name. Dr. Hogg worked primarily with gay young offenders who had been referred to him by the courts. He thought that it might be useful to set up a weekly discussion meeting of six or eight gay men, self-accepting or not, to just sit around and talk about what it meant to be gay. Dr. Hogg wanted to sit in on the discussion as an observer, just to listen and not to criticize or express doubt. I agreed to arrange for the group to meet.

At that time I had an older gay friend named John Harvey, and he agreed to host these discussions at his home in East York. I lined up about six other fellows who were gay, of various types, and we started meeting for a couple of hours on Wednesday evenings. This continued for a few months until June 1964, when Jack and I decided to leave Toronto.

These meetings were really very interesting. Dr. Hogg arrived, was friendly, and didn't indicate in any way where he stood on the subject of homosexuality. We all knew he was a psychiatrist, but he said he was not there to evaluate us. He just wanted to hear what gay people talked about, and to see what kind of people we were. Dr. Hogg had never met any gay men other than youngsters who were in dire straits with the law. So the group sat around and talked about a great many things, but mainly about homosexuality. We talked about the state of the gay world in Toronto, and what the police were up to, and about love affairs that had come and gone. I remember that one of the guys in the group was really mixed-up. He was a young x-ray technician at a local hospital. He knew that he was gay but didn't like it at all, and we used to talk to him quite a bit.

One evening Dr. Hogg was accompanied by a handsome kid about seventeen years old, who was one of his patients. He seemed absolutely petrified with fear. He sat as far away as possible from the rest of us, listening to what was going on but not contributing anything. He never said a word all night. On another occasion, Dr. Hogg arrived with a man, about forty, whom he introduced as a colleague. This person sat in absolute frozen-faced indignation throughout the entire evening.

In June 1964 I announced to the group that the next week would be the last meeting, as I was moving away. Dr. Hogg felt that was fine. We had been meeting for awhile and the group had served its purpose. Dr. Hogg suggested that we hold a little party after our final meeting, and we agreed. We brought bottles of wine and snacks. Just as the party was winding down, and everyone was preparing to leave, Dr. Hogg announced to the group how much he had enjoyed listening to the conversations. He had learned a great deal about what it meant to be a self-accepting gay man. Before he had attended the meetings, he had dealt with homosexuality as a social problem for years, and had explored the various current theories on cause and cure, and so on. The meetings had opened his eyes, because until then he had never met well-adjusted gay men. I must admit that I found his reaction rewarding, which made the experience of the discussion group even more worthwhile[9].

During the first half of 1964 I kept very busy, with work, activism, and meetings. I was not entirely happy, though, due to my separation from Jack, and to my perception of a lack of support for gay activism within the gay community itself.

Although Jack and I separated early in 1964 after more than fifteen years together, the split was not complete. I must admit that during the separation we still saw each other regularly for sex. But it just wasn't the same. I longed for the relationship to come back, to be viable again. I had made up my mind when I was about twenty-five that I was going to meet someone, I was going to fall in love with him, and we were going to grow old together as a couple and die together. After my separation from Jack, I saw this starting to slip away.

At the same time, I began to be disenchanted with being a gay activist. I was pissed off that most members of the gay community in Toronto didn't give a hoot about what came to be known as "gay liberation." You must remember that when Jack and I met, and for years afterward, the mere act of two men going to bed together was a serious criminal offence in Canada. This was the case for every gay couple. We could have been declared criminal sexual psychopaths if we'd been caught at it, and sentenced to an indeterminate prison sentence. Although the law didn't stop any of us from going to bed, not very many people were prepared to state publicly that the law was wrong, or to actively protest for change.

I want to clarify that I wasn't looking for adulation from the gay community for espousing the cause. More support would have been nice, though. I remember sitting one night in the Music Room, early in 1964 after my split with Jack, when my letters and articles were being published in the mainstream press — in the *Toronto Daily Star*, *Saturday Night*, and so on. This guy about thirty years old came over and said that someone had pointed me out as being Jim Egan. He introduced himself and said that he had read a letter of mine in the paper the other night and thought it was really great. He was so glad that someone was standing up for the gay community. I thanked him, appreciating the kind word, but said it would be a better if he were to take a couple of minutes and write a letter to the editor and thank him for publishing my letter. He looked as though I'd stabbed him! He became very nervous and scuttled away. This was the sort of passivity in the community that infuriated me. Why wouldn't a man thirty years old have the courage to write a letter to the editor and thank him for publishing Jim Egan's letter? I was becoming disillusioned with the congratulations I received for my activities, but no real support. The letters and articles I wrote took a considerable amount of my time, and I began to feel that they

Gay (later *Gay International*), Toronto's first gay tabloid, began publication in 1964.

Two magazine was launched in Toronto in 1964 by Gayboy Publishing; Egan contributed to *Two*.

accomplished little other than to let the editor and the occasional reader know that homophobic attitudes were not acceptable. I know this may sound like sour grapes, but it's what I felt.

After our separation Jack was having a hard time, too. He missed me. Jack had a sister, who was about twenty years older, and they were extremely close. She was absolutely furious when we split up. She was more angry with Jack than with me, and bugged him constantly and insisted that we get back together again. She couldn't believe that we'd separated after fifteen years.

One night in May 1964 Jack and I met, by coincidence, at the Parkside Tavern [located at 530 Yonge Street]. He invited me back to our old apartment and we had a long, long talk. I finally said to Jack that I wanted to get back into the relationship and that I was prepared to abandon my gay activism. But I told him we'd have to leave Toronto or else I'd surely be drawn back into it again. It was time for a fresh start. He agreed, and we discussed the idea of moving either to New Zealand or British Columbia. In those days it was easy to emigrate to New Zealand. But in my biology business I had done a lot of work for a company in Victoria that retailed biological specimens to schools and universities. So I wrote to the owner of the company and told him we were thinking of moving to British Columbia and getting into the wholesale end of marine biological specimens. I asked him what he thought of the idea, and he replied in a highly enthusiastic letter urging us to do that.

So we decided to settle in British Columbia. The first thing we did was recombine our bank accounts. We had some money from the proceeds of the sale of our property near Beamsville, and the business that I was operating was doing quite well. We bought a brand new five-ton truck chassis and had a used furniture van body mounted on the back. We hired two meaty young men from the Salvation Army, and they helped us pack the truck with all of our possessions. The truck was just barely big enough to hold everything. Our huge old apartment was a monstrous place full of stuff, but we were able to pack it all in. Then, one day in June 1964, we left Toronto for a new life, driving all across Canada with this big truck, and three chihuahuas sitting on the seat between us[10].

Afterword

Jim Egan kept his promise to Jack Nesbit for more than twenty years. Except for the occasional outburst, such as a letter-writing campaign in 1973 disputing two homophobic columns in the Victoria *Daily Colonist* written by Gorde Hunter, Jim was not involved in gay issues again until 1985[1]. In fact, Jim and Jack had no significant gay contact at all from late 1964 to 1985.

They drove across Canada and arrived on Vancouver Island in July 1964. They didn't know people there, and were relieved to be out of Toronto's gay swirl. Jim and Jack settled in the town of Duncan and set about establishing the Jamack Biological Supply Company, a wholesale business specializing in marine specimens such as starfish and sea cucumbers. Working as a team, they perfected the preservation of these animals in their natural state. Within a year they had more business than they could handle, but decided to keep Jamack as a small, two-man operation.

Jim soon developed a great interest in the environmental movement then starting to blossom in British Columbia. He joined the Society for the Prevention of Environmental Collapse (SPEC), one of the leading groups of the day. Jim became vice-president of the Cowichan Valley branch of SPEC, and his passion for environmental issues continues to this day.

In 1968 Jim and Jack moved to Thetis Island, where they purchased waterfront property on Telegraph Harbour that included a small, comfortable house. They built a lab there to continue their thriving business. The collection of marine specimens for preservation involves hard physical work, including scrambling over slippery rocks on the beach and carrying heavy pails of water. By 1970 Jack's back started to give out, and in 1972 Jim and Jack decided to give up their business. They sold the property on Thetis Island and moved to Chemainus, B.C., where they lived in a rented cabin.

Life at Chemainus was quiet. They lounged around and enjoyed their retirement. During the summer Jim involved himself in environmental work while Jack indulged his passion for gardening. At the first sign of winter they packed up a trailer and drove to Arizona or California. Their life as Snowbirds was short-lived, though. They became restless, sold the truck and trailer, and decided to visit India, where they spent three months backpacking around the country.

In 1974 Jim and Jack moved again. They bought a property at

Jim and Jack in British Columbia, ca. 1972.

Merville, on which they built a two-thousand-square-foot stackwall house. In his spare time Jack worked at the local crisis centre, first on the telephone lines and later as a marriage counsellor. Jim worked as a free-lance carpenter and did environmental work. In 1980 he became embroiled in an environmental controversy. The local sewage plant had proposed to the Waste Management Branch of the British Columbia Ministry of the Environment that the raw sewage it collected from Comox, Courtenay, and CFB Comox be pumped out, untreated, into the Strait of Georgia. Egan became a member of the Save Our Straits Committee, an ad hoc group of local environmentalists devoted to blocking this plan. The protests of the Save Our Straits Committee went into high gear when the Ministry granted the permit to the plant. The Committee was eventually successful in overturning the permit and persuaded the Ministry to require the plant to treat the sewage.

Jim's environmental work made him a local celebrity, and in 1981 he was encouraged to stand as a candidate for regional director for Electoral Area B of the Regional District of Comox-Strathcona. Egan was reluctant at first, but decided to run and was elected. His election was a first — Jim Egan was the first openly gay man living in an openly gay relationship to be elected to public office in Canada. Egan had a distinguished career as a regional director and took a prominent role in lobbying efforts to acquire the land that eventually became Seal Bay Park. He was re-elected twice. Jim served from 1981 until 1993 when, at the age of seventy-two, he decided not to stand for re-election.

In May 1985 Jim and Jack sold their property at Merville and moved into a bungalow on the outskirts of Courtenay. Soon after the move they began to meet local gay people. During their life in British Columbia Jim and Jack had not had gay friends. They had developed a network of heterosexual friends who gradually came to understand the nature of their relationship. Some friends asked if they were a couple, and Jim and Jack talked openly about their relationship. Other friends never asked, and Jim and Jack never told.

By the 1980s Jack's attitude toward gay liberation had changed, and in the fall of 1985 he and Jim started the Comox Valley branch of the Island Gay Society. They placed an advertisement in the personal column of the Saturday editions of the *Times-Colonist* announcing a gay information line. Soon they were sponsoring a drop-in at their home once a month, which sometimes attracted as many as thirty

The stackwall house at Merville, B.C., ca. 1976.

people. The drop-in continued for eleven years, after which time Jim and Jack decided they had contributed enough. The Comox Valley branch of the Island Gay Society collapsed soon after. During part of this time Jim was also involved with the North Island AIDS Coalition; he served as president in 1994.

In the late 1980s and early 1990s Jim Egan and Jack Nesbit were thrust into the public eye by their Supreme Court challenge, in which they used the Canadian Charter of Rights and Freedoms to challenge the discriminatory exclusion of pension benefits to same-sex couples under the Old Age Security Act. Theirs was the first claim involving same-sex rights heard by the Supreme Court of Canada under the Charter, which guarantees that all Canadians are to receive equal benefit of the law.

The background for the case started in 1975, when the spousal allowance benefit was introduced under section 19(1) of the Old Age Security Act. In section 2 of the Act, and in dozens of other pieces of federal legislation, the word "spouse" was defined as a person of the opposite sex. This meant that same-sex couples, even those who had been together for many years, were ineligible for any of the tax breaks, benefits, and allowances heterosexuals could obtain, even a common law couple who had been together for only one year. This despite the fact that all Canadians — gay or heterosexual — throughout their working lives pay income tax at a rate established by the federal government that allows the government to pay out all these tax breaks and tax benefits.

When Canadians become sixty-four years of age they apply for the old age pension. They receive their first pension cheque the month after they turn sixty-five. If their partner, either the husband or wife, is sixty years of age and if their combined income is less than a certain amount, the younger partner can apply for spousal benefits, which the government instituted to aid the couple until the younger member is old enough to receive the old age pension.

It was obvious to Jim and Jack that the exclusion of same-sex couples from eligibility for these benefits constituted a blatant case of discrimination. On 25 February 1987, when Jack was about to turn sixty, they applied for the spousal benefit on his behalf, with the full expectation that the request would be denied. Jim and Jack didn't really care about the extra income the spousal benefit would provide. Their goal was to fight institutionalized discrimination against gay people. The application and expected refusal were just a hook on which to hang a court challenge under the Charter. Their goal was to force a high court interpretation of section 15 of the Canadian Charter of Rights and Freedoms that would prohibit discrimination on the basis of sexual orientation. The words "sexual orientation" did not appear in the list of prohibited grounds for discrimination under section 15, but many constitutional lawyers believed that it was an analogous ground and could be read into the Charter without requiring a formal amendment. If the high court ruled in their favour, same-sex couples would be legally recognized as spouses and would be protected from discrimination in all areas of federal legislation.

When Jack was refused the spousal benefit by Health and Welfare Canada only one week later, the couple hired Victoria lawyer David Vickers, of Vickers and Palmer, who approached the Court Challenges Program, which is sponsored by the Canadian Council on Social Development and is funded by the federal government. This program was established to provide funds to support the cost of litigation in selected test cases related to equality rights issues under the Charter. Their application was successful, and Egan and Nesbit brought an action in the Trial Division of the Federal Court of Canada on 6 December 1988. The action appealed Health and Welfare Canada's ruling and claimed discrimination under the Old Age Security Act in its definition of the word "spouse." They also asked the court to rule that the definition of "spouse" in the legislation was unconstitutional in that it discriminated against same-sex couples on the basis of gender and sexual orientation (an analogous ground), contrary to section 15(1) of the Canadian Charter of Rights and Freedoms. It is important to note that in using the Charter to challenge the legislation, Jim and Jack did not request special rights, special protection, special privileges, or special benefits, just absolute equality under the law.

After months of delays the case was finally heard in Vancouver on 28-29 May 1991, and on 2 December 1991 Justice Leonard Martin delivered his decision: he dismissed the action. He ruled that although the Old Age Security Act did not define same-sex partners as spouses, it did not discriminate on the basis of gender or sexual orientation. Martin stated that same-sex couples "do not fall within the meaning of the word 'spouse' any more than heterosexual couples who live together and do not publicly represent themselves as man and wife, such as brother and sister, brother and brother,

sister and sister, two relatives, two friends, or parent and child."
Martin concluded that Egan and Nesbit were not the sort of couple
Parliament had in mind when the Act was passed in 1975, that "... the
relationship is a different one than a spousal relationship and that the
parties to such relationship cannot expect to share the benefits
accorded to those in spousal relationships, not because of their sexual
orientation, but because their relationship is not a spousal one[2]."

Jim and Jack decided to appeal this ruling. Their lawyer, David
Vickers, had been elevated to the Supreme Court of British Columbia,
and their case was taken up by Victoria lawyer Joseph Arvay, of
Arvay, Finlay and Associates. The Court Challenges Program agreed
to fund an appeal. Unfortunately, the program was cancelled by the
Mulroney government. Arvay agreed to waive his fee. He sent the
case to the Federal Court of Appeal on 12 August 1992. In their
appeal Egan and Nesbit focussed on whether the restrictive
definition of "spouse" in the Old Age Security Act violated section
15(1) of the Charter on the basis of discrimination based on sexual
orientation. On 29 April 1993 Egan and Nesbit lost again when
Canada's second-highest court upheld the judgment, ruling in a 2-1
decision that Egan and Nesbit had not been discriminated against
based on their sexual orientation. Justice Allen Linden, in the only
dissenting opinion, stated that pension benefits should be extended
to same-sex couples who meet the other requirements, and that to
deny such benefits promotes "the prejudiced view of the legitimacy
and worth of these relationships[3]."

Egan and Nesbit were prepared to fight all the way to the
Supreme Court of Canada and were supported in their endeavour by
the reinstituted Court Challenges Program. On 2 June 1993 Joseph
Arvay filed an application to appeal to the Supreme Court, and the
appeal was heard on 1 November 1994.

The Supreme Court appeal hinged on two questions: "1) Does
the definition of 'spouse' in section 2 of the Old Age Security Act,
R.S.C., 1985, chapter O-9, infringe or deny section 15(1) of the
Canadian Charter of Rights and Freedoms?; and 2) If the answer to
question 1 is yes, is the infringement or denial demonstrably justified
in a free and democratic society pursuant to section 1 of the Canadian
Charter of Rights and Freedoms?" The judgment of the Supreme
Court of Canada in the case of *Egan and Nesbit v. Canada* was rendered
on 25 May 1995, more than eight years after Jack had applied for the

spousal benefit and more than six years after they had introduced an action in the Federal Court of Canada. In a 5-4 decision, the appeal was dismissed.

The result was bittersweet for Egan and Nesbit. It was a victory of sorts because the court agreed 5-4 that the current definition of "spouse" in the Old Age Security Act was discriminatory. This decision was a substantial step forward for gays and lesbians: it was the first time the Supreme Court had ruled that the failure of federal legislation to recognize same-sex relationships is discriminatory. All nine justices also held that "sexual orientation" must be read into the Charter as a ground of discrimination analogous to existing grounds such as race, gender, and religion. But the Court also ruled 5-4 that the discrimination was justified under section 1 of the Charter. Four justices ruled that section 15 does not extend to same-sex relationships. Justice John Sopinka cast the deciding vote when he ruled that although the failure to recognize same-sex relationships is discriminatory, this particular piece of legislation can be justified because the Government of Canada is entitled to take time to bring its laws into conformity with the Charter[4].

Jim and Jack's immediate reaction to the decision is captured in David Adkin's documentary "Jim Loves Jack: The James Egan Story." Surprise and disappointment are etched on their faces. Jack suffered three angina attacks from the stress of the situation. Jim later referred to the decision as a "black cloud with a silver lining."

Gay and lesbian individuals and groups across the country expressed dismay with the decision, but there was optimism concerning implications of the case. Some comments were particularly astute. Equality for Gays and Lesbians Everywhere (EGALE) saw the case "a loss but not a defeat." EGALE's solicitor, Cynthia Peterson, stated that as a result of the ruling that sexual orientation constitutes a ground of discrimination, "Every Canadian statute which treats same-sex relationships as inferior to heterosexual relationships is therefore subject to constitutional challenge." She continued, "The Supreme Court has left the door open for future legal challenges. This is only the beginning and there is no question that the Courts are moving forward. The only question that remains is whether the Government will recognize our right to equality, or whether it will continue to pour millions of dollars of taxpayers' money into defending unjust laws[5]."

Jim and Jack were hailed as heroes after the ruling in *Egan and*

Jim and Jack as grand marshals of the Toronto Pride parade, 1995. Photo by
Ali Kazimi.

Nesbit v. Canada. They had done their share in fighting for same-sex equality rights. During the rest of 1995 and into 1996 their story was told on radio, television, in numerous newspaper articles, and eventually in the documentary "Jim Loves Jack." Jim received a national human rights award in Ottawa on 28 May 1995, presented by the Lambda Foundation for Excellence. Jim and Jack were the honorary parade marshals at both the Toronto and Vancouver Pride events in 1995. On 2 June 1996 Jim was invited to Victoria to address a conference of Canadian human rights commissioners, sponsored by the British Columbia Human Rights Commission. And, in September 1997, Jim was awarded a Paul Harris Fellowship, the highest award bestowed by Rotary International, in recognition of his community service.

Jim and Jack still live in Courtenay, enjoying retirement and looking forward to celebrating their fiftieth anniversary on 23 August 1998. Although recently slowed by illness, they continue to show a keen interest in gay liberation and do what they can to support the fight for same-sex benefits. Jim still gives interviews and attends conferences. For example, he offered insightful comments at the plenary session entitled "Not a Faggoty Dress-up Party: Disrobing the Supreme Court of Canada in the Post-Egan Era," part of the national gay, lesbian, bisexual, and transgendered conference Queering the Nation at York University on 27 June 1998. In his seventy-seventh year Egan remains a contender, fighting the good fight and instilling in a younger generation the importance of challenging the conspiracy of silence.

Don McLeod
Toronto, July 1998

Notes

Preface

1. As Gary Kinsman has noted, "Mainstream psychiatry and psychology in the twentieth century have generally viewed homosexuality as a symptom of 'infantile regression' or some other pathological disorder, and have developed various strategies to cure, regulate, or adjust patients to the heterosexual norm." See Gary Kinsman, *The Regulation of Desire: Homo and Hetero Sexualities,* 2nd ed., rev. (Montréal: Black Rose Books, 1996), p. 31. For an examination of psychoanalysis and homosexuality see Kenneth Lewes, *The Psychoanalytic Theory of Male Homosexuality* (New York: Simon and Schuster, 1988); see also Vern L. Bullough, *Science in the Bedroom: A History of Sex Research* (New York: Basic Books, 1994).

2. For general background on social conditions for gay men in Toronto during the 1940s and 1950s see David Stewart Churchill, "Coming Out in a Cold Climate: A History of Gay Men in Toronto during the 1950s" (Master of Arts thesis, Graduate Department of Education, University of Toronto, 1993); Paul Jackson, "'Male Lovers' in Canada, 1930-1950: Breaking the Code of Silence" (Master of Arts paper, Department of History, Queen's University, 1994); and Kinsman, *The Regulation of Desire*, 2nd ed., rev., especially chapter seven. See also John Grube, "'No More Shit': The Struggle for Democratic Gay Space in Toronto," in *Queers in Space: Communities, Public Places, Sites of Resistance*, eds. Gordon Brent Ingram, Anne-Marie Bouthillette, and Yolanda Retter (Seattle: Bay Press, 1997), pp. 127-45; and John Grube, "Queens and Flaming Virgins: Towards a Sense of Gay Community," *Rites*, March 1986, pp. 14-17. For a study of male-male intimacy in Toronto during an earlier period see Steven Maynard, "'Horrible Temptations': Sex, Men, and Working-Class Male Youth in Urban Ontario, 1890-1935," *Canadian Historical Review* 78 (June 1997): 191-235. For an examination of the anti-gay discrimination campaign conducted by the Canadian state during the 1950s through the 1970s see Gary Kinsman and Patrizia Gentile, with the assistance of Heidi McDonell and Mary Mahood-Greer, *"In the Interests of the State": The Anti-gay, Anti-lesbian National Security Campaign in Canada: A Preliminary Research Report* (Sudbury, Ont.: Laurentian University, 1998).

3. Amendments to the Canadian Criminal Code passed in Bill C-150 came into effect on 26 August 1969, decriminalizing "gross indecency" and "buggery" in private between two consenting adults twenty-one years of age or older. This change in the law no doubt acted as a spur to gay organizing in Toronto, although there had earlier been at least one failed attempt to establish a homophile group there. See Donald W. McLeod, *Lesbian and Gay Liberation in Canada: A Selected Annotated Chronology, 1964-1975* (Toronto: ECW Press/Homewood Books, 1996), pp. 10-11, 41-44. For information on the rise of a gay liberation movement in Canada, see Kinsman, *The Regulation*

of Desire, 2nd ed., rev., particularly chapters eight and nine; and McLeod, *Lesbian and Gay Liberation in Canada*.

4. The case of *Egan and Nesbit v. Canada* is well documented in Donald G. Casswell, *Lesbians, Gay Men, and Canadian Law* (Toronto: Emond Montgomery Publications, 1996), pp. 371-411. See also Robert Wintemute, "Discrimination against Same-Sex Couples: Sections 15(1) and 1 of the *Charter: Egan v. Canada,*" *Canadian Bar Review* 74 (December 1995): 682-713; Robert Wintemute, *Sexual Orientation and Human Rights: The United States Constitution, the European Convention, and The Canadian Charter* (Oxford: Clarendon Press, 1995), pp. 254-60; and John A. Yogis, Randall R. Duplak, and J. Royden Trainor, *Sexual Orientation and Canadian Law: An Assessment of the Law Affecting Lesbian and Gay Persons* (Toronto: Emond Montgomery Publications, 1995), pp. 21-24.

5. Alfred Taylor [pseud. of Philip McLeod], "A Perfect Beginner: Jim Egan and the Tabloids," *Canadian Lesbian and Gay History Network Newsletter*, no. 2 (1986), pp. 12-18.

6. Robert Champagne (interviewing Jim Egan), "Canada's Pioneer Gay Activist: Jim Egan," *Rites*, December 1986-January 1987, pp. 12-14; *Jim Egan: Canada's Pioneer Gay Activist*, compiled and introduced by Robert Champagne, Canadian Lesbian and Gay History Network Publication, no. 1 (Toronto: Canadian Lesbian and Gay History Network, 1987).

7. Gary Kinsman, *The Regulation of Desire: Sexuality in Canada* (Montréal: Black Rose Books, 1987), pp. 119-120, 160. A second, revised edition was published as *The Regulation of Desire: Homo and Hetero Sexualities* by the same publisher in 1996; see pp. 167-69 and 251-52.

8. Churchill, "Coming Out in a Cold Climate."

9. David Adkin, "Jim Loves Jack: The James Egan Story." (Toronto: David Adkin Productions, Inc., 1996), 53 minutes.

10. Michael Riordon, *Out Our Way: Gay and Lesbian Life in the Country* (Toronto: Between the Lines, 1996), pp. 106-110.

Chapter One: Beginnings

No notes.

Chapter Two: Wartime and After: Gaining Gay Experience

1. Dr. Raymond Crandall Parker (1903-1974) had a long and distinguished career in the field of virology. Today he is best remembered for his work with polio. Parker was directly responsible for developing the culture technique

that made possible the mass production of the Salk polio vaccine. See "Raymond Crandall Parker," *The Canadian Who's Who*, Vol. 13, 1973-75 (Toronto: Who's Who Canadian Publications, 1975), p. 779; "Report of the Honorary Secretary for the Year 1962-63," *Proceedings and Transactions of the Royal Society of Canada,* Fourth ser., vol. 1. Meeting of June, 1963 (Ottawa: Royal Society of Canada, 1963), p. 54.

2. Dr. Alexis Carrel (1873-1944) was renowned for developing innovative surgical techniques and for studies in tissue culture. In 1912 he was awarded the Nobel Prize for Physiology or Medicine for developing a method of suturing blood vessels. Carrel worked at the Rockefeller Institute for Medical Research from 1919 to 1941. See Theodore I. Malinin, *Surgery and Life: The Extraordinary Career of Alexis Carrel* (New York: Harcourt Brace Jovanovich, 1979).

3. Raymond Crandall Parker, *Methods of Tissue Culture* (New York: P.B. Hoeber, 1938; 3rd ed., 1961). This work included a foreword by Alexis Carrel.

4. After he left Connaught Laboratories Egan discovered that Dr. Parker was gay. Egan recalls, "I never had a clue about this all the time I was working with him in the lab."

5. Allan Bérubé, *Coming Out Under Fire: The History of Gay Men and Women in World War Two* (New York: The Free Press, 1990).

6. John Horne Burns, *The Gallery* (New York: Harper, 1947).

Chapter Three: Living the Gay Life in Post-War Toronto

1. After Egan met Jack Nesbit, Jack and Charlie Egan became very close friends, and remain so to this day.

2. Gore Vidal, *The City and the Pillar* (New York: Dutton, 1948).

3. Jim Egan and Jack Nesbit were monogamous for more than twenty years, at which point they decided that monogamy was not vital to their relationship. As Jim recalls, "Although I don't think either one of us had more than four or five subsequent extracurricular experiences, it was clearly understood that these would only take place where there was no threat to our relationship. There never was. I can say that over the years, like any couple, Jack and I have had arguments and disagreements, but never over a third person."

Chapter Four: Challenging the Conspiracy of Silence: Jim Egan's Emergence As a Gay Activist during the 1950s

1. For a discussion of these and other gay cruising sites in Toronto during the

1950s, see Churchill, "Coming Out in a Cold Climate," particularly chapter three, "Urban Spaces and Gay Sites," pp. 55-75. Toronto has a long and remarkable history of police entrapment of gay men that merits systematic study. Much of this history is still hidden away in accounts of arrests published in mainstream and tabloid newspapers, and, more recently, in the gay press, and in personal accounts or oral histories. For a study on Toronto police surveillance and entrapment early in this century see Steven Maynard, "Through a Hole in the Lavatory Wall: Homosexual Subcultures, Police Surveillance, and the Dialectics of Discovery: Toronto, 1890-1930," *Journal of the History of Sexuality* 5 (October 1994): 207-42. In researching this project I have examined numerous published accounts of police entrapment, many of which relate to High Park. See, for example, an account of events at "the most famous pervert-trap in Toronto" in Ron Haggart, "The Strange Ordeal of Malcolm Phlarb," *Toronto Daily Star*, night ed., 19 July 1961, p. 7; and Ron Haggart, "Malcolm Phlarb's Ordeal in the Weird Washroom," *Toronto Daily Star*, night ed., 20 July 1961, p. 7.

2. I have been able to examine all issues of *Justice Weekly* published during the 1950s. This tabloid was adept at reporting local arrests of homosexuals, and is useful for tracking the vigorous police campaigns of entrapment and arrest of gay men during this period. For example, the following small selection of articles details the arrests of more than one hundred men in High Park and several locations in downtown Toronto: "Magistrates Are Not Helping Police Rounding Up High Park Sex Deviates: Fines Are Being Imposed for Revolting Practices in Washrooms for Public," *Justice Weekly*, 9 April 1955, pp. 3, 5, 16; "University of Toronto Grounds Attract Homos: Two More Jailed, Fined," *Justice Weekly*, 30 July 1956, pp. 2, 4; "Old Hole-in-Wall Technique Employed in Homosexual Orgies in Public Park: Seventeen Sex Diviates [sic] Convicted in Short Time, Fine Is $100 or 15 Days," *Justice Weekly*, 3 November 1956, pp. 2, 4; "Police Express Concern Over Homos' Activities: Large Number Arrested," *Justice Weekly*, 24 November 1956, pp. 3, 11; "One Hundred Homosexuals Arrested in Toronto during Last Three Months: All Tried Found Guilty of Gross Indecency; Two Policemen Given Credit," *Justice Weekly*, 2 February 1957, pp. 2, 16; "Intensive Police Drive against Homos: Thirteen Are Rounded Up in Restaurant on Yonge; Eight Pay Fines of $100," *Justice Weekly*, 15 March 1958, p. 12; "Director of Hospitalization Among Homos Admitting Gross Indecency; Back to High Park from Honey Dew," *Justice Weekly*, 26 April 1958, pp. 3, 14; and "Men's Lavatory in Movie Theatre Is New Hang-out for Homosexuals: Gross Indecency Charges Admitted by Four Arrested; Two Accused Get Remands," *Justice Weekly*, 21 February 1959, pp. 3, 5.

    For an examination of the treatment of gay men in *Hush Free Press*, another Toronto tabloid of the period, see Eric Setliff, "Sex Fiend or Swish Kid? Gay Men in *Hush Free Press*, 1946-1956" (Master of Arts paper, Department of History, University of Toronto, 1994); and Eric Setliff, "Sex Fiends or Swish Kids? Gay Men in *Hush Free Press*, 1946-1956," in *Gendered Pasts: Historical Essays on Femininity and Masculinity in Canada*, eds. Kathryn

McPherson, Cecilia Morgan, and Nancy Forestell (Toronto: Oxford University Press, forthcoming).

3. Alfred C. Kinsey, Wardell B. Pomeroy, and Clyde E. Martin, *Sexual Behavior in the Human Male* (Philadelphia: W.B. Saunders Company, 1948). Kinsey's famous study appeared just at the beginning of what has been described as a "sex crime panic" that swept the United States (and Canada) from roughly 1949 to 1955. One of the results of this panic was the transformation of the public image of the homosexual from a harmless "fairy" to a sexual psychopath or dangerous child molester. See George Chauncey, Jr., "The Postwar Sex Crime Panic," in *True Stories from the American Past*, ed. William Graebner (New York: McGraw-Hill, 1993), pp. 160-78; Estelle B. Freedman, "'Uncontrolled Desires': The Response to the Sexual Psychopath, 1920-1960," in *Passion and Power: Sexuality in History*, eds. Kathy Peiss and Christina Simmons, with Robert A. Padgug (Philadelphia: Temple University Press, 1989), pp. 199-225; and Eric Setliff, "Sex Fiend or Swish Kid? Gay Men in *Hush Free Press*, 1946-1956" (Master of Arts paper), pp. 1-3.

4. Allen Churchill, "What Is a Homosexual?" *Argosy*, August 1949, pp. 28-29, 96-97.

5. Ralph H. Major, Jr., "New Moral Menace to Our Youth," *Coronet*, September 1950, pp. 101-102.

6. See Appendix D, "The Correspondence of Jim Egan, 1950-1964."

7. James Egan, "Views Vary on the Kinsey Report: For Publication" (letter), *Globe and Mail*, final ed., 16 May 1950, p. 6.

8. For overviews of the top Canadian tabloids of the day see H.R. How, "Half a Million for Sex and Scandal," *Canadian Business*, July 1951, pp. 34-35, 66; and Frank Rasky, "Canada's Scandalous Scandal Sheets," *Liberty*, November 1954, pp. 17, 74-76, 78-80. See also Gary Kinsman's analysis of the tabloids in his *The Regulation of Desire*, 2nd ed., rev., p. 168.

9. "Unparalleled Orgies of Perversion Exposed by Intrepid *Flash* Reporter: Toronto Steam Bath Uncovered as Den for Unnatural Vice!," *Flash*, 2 May 1950, p. 5.

10. J.L.E., "Reader Defends Homos, Says They're Inverts" (letter), *Flash*, 16 May 1950, pp. 16, ?. For an analysis of this and other articles and letters by Egan published in the Toronto tabloids see Alfred Taylor [pseud. of Philip McLeod], "A Perfect Beginner: Jim Egan and the Tabloids."

11. Donald Webster Cory [pseud. of Edward Sagarin], *The Homosexual in America: A Subjective Approach* (New York: Greenberg, 1951).

12. J.L.E., "*TNT* Taken to Task by ????" (letter), *True News Times (TNT)*, 16 October 1950, p. 11.

13. For a brief analysis of these columns see Churchill, "Coming Out in a Cold Climate," pp. 51-54.

14. Sara H. Carleton, "The Truth About Homosexuals," *Sir!*, June 1950, p. 57.

15. Leo Engle [pseud. of Jim Egan], "I Am a Homosexual," *Sir!*, December 1950, p. ?.

16. J.L.E., "Fairy Nice" (letter), *True News Times (TNT)*, 19 February 1951, p. ?.

17. See "Appendix B: A Checklist of Publications by Jim Egan, 1950-1964."

18. Philip Daniels was a busy man during the early 1950s. Not only did he write, edit, and publish a weekly newspaper, he also worked full-time as a cashier at the Long Branch Racetrack in Toronto. Daniels was born in England in about 1893. After emigrating to Canada in 1911 he worked as a professional boxer, promoter, and sports writer popularly known as "Darkey" Daniels. During the Great War he served with the Canadian Expeditionary Force and edited an army paper, *The Siberian Bugle*. After the war Daniels continued his career in journalism, working as the editor of such publications as *Canadian Sports and Daily Racing Form*. During World War Two Sergeant-Major Daniels was the editor of *The Bullet*, the official weekly army newspaper for Military District No. 2 and Camp Borden. At this time Daniels became involved with the Toronto tabloids, and in 1945 was briefly the editor of *Flash*. Late that year Daniels decided to form *Justice Weekly* as an alternative to the other local tabloids, which he felt were more interested in making money than in exposing the truth or working for "justice." *Justice Weekly* began publication the first week of January 1946 and continued until 15 April 1972. See "Introducing Ourselves," *Justice Weekly*, 5 January 1946, p. 4; and Rasky, "Canada's Scandalous Scandal Sheets," p. 80.

19. George Hislop recalls that these two establishments were also known as "the Chamber of Commerce and the Board of Trade," because of the number of male hustlers there and due to their proximity to Bay Street, the heart of Toronto's financial district. For more information on the Corners, see Churchill, "Coming Out in a Cold Climate," pp. 81-84, 88, 90.

20. Philip Daniels once outlined his feelings about homosexuality in an article in *Justice Weekly*: "... 'Justice' carries articles on homosexuals because I believe in throwing my columns open to everybody. Homosexuality has become an engrossing theme the world over judging by recent happenings, as for instance the appointment of the Wolfenden committee and its most interesting report. I am not a homosexual, nor do I condone their way of living. At the same time I do not condemn them, that is as long as they stay

among themselves and leave heterosexuals alone. And I do believe in presenting their side of the story. That is what a newspaper is for — or should be." See Phil Daniels, "Here Is Answer to Unfair, Untrue Article," *Justice Weekly*, 21 March 1959, p. 16.

21. See "Appendix B: A Checklist of Publications by Jim Egan, 1950-1964."

22. The arrests of Gielgud, Lord Montagu, and others for homosexual offenses led to a wave of public commentary on homosexuality in England and elsewhere during 1953-54. See Stephen Jeffery-Poulter, *Peers, Queers, and Commons: The Struggle for Gay Law Reform from 1950 to the Present* (London: Routledge, 1991), pp. 14-19.

23. See "Appendix B: A Checklist of Publications by Jim Egan, 1950-1964."

24. [Jim Egan], "Parliamentary Legislative Committee Ignored This Letter from Homosexual Suggesting Changes in Criminal Code," *Justice Weekly*, 19 March 1955, pp. 5, 14.

25. From 1954 through 1960 *Justice Weekly* reprinted a great deal of material from the gay press. I have studied all of the issues published during this period and counted 240 items (including parts of serialized articles), mostly from *ONE Magazine* and *The Mattachine Review*. During 1956 alone fifty-one items appeared, an average of one per issue.

26. Based in San Francisco, Harold L. (Hal) Call (1917-) became the head of The Mattachine Society in 1953. In 1954 he co-founded Pan-Graphic Press (with Donald Lucas), and in 1955 began publication of *The Mattachine Review*. See "'Gay Sexualist'— Hal Call," in Eric Marcus, *Making History: The Struggle for Gay and Lesbian Equal Rights, 1945-1990. An Oral History* (New York: HarperCollins Publishers, 1992), pp. 59-69.

27. W. Dorr Legg (1904-1994) was the Administrative Director of ONE, Incorporated, from its beginning in 1952. For more than four decades he was remarkably prolific as a leading American gay activist, educator, and writer. See "40 Year Dedicated Activist Dorr Legg Dies at 89," *ONE/IGLA Bulletin*, no. 1 (1995), p. 4.

28. Much like Egan, Henry Gerber (1892-1972) was a lone pioneer whose early vision of gay rights would be fulfilled by a later generation. See Jim Coughenour, "The Life and Times of an Ordinary Hero: Henry Gerber's Fight for Freedom — 45 Years Before Stonewall," *Windy City Times*, 22 June 1989, sec. 2, pp. 60, 62; *Encyclopedia of Homosexuality*, s.v. "Gerber, Henry," by Warren Johansson; and Henry Gerber, "The Society for Human Rights — 1925," *ONE Magazine*, September 1962, pp. 5-11.

29. For an account of the conference see D.S., "Mental Health and Homosexuality," *ONE Magazine*, April 1959, pp. 15-16. Jim Kepner (1923-

1997) was a pioneer gay activist, writer, and archivist. In 1942 he founded the collection that eventually formed the basis for the International Gay and Lesbian Archives, the largest gay and lesbian resource centre in the world, now housed at the University of Southern California, Los Angeles. See David W. Dunlap, "Jim Kepner, in 70's, Is Dead: Historian of Gay Rights Effort," *New York Times*, late ed., 20 November 1997, p. B13; and "News Hound — Jim Kepner," in Marcus, *Making History*, pp. 43-53. A selection of Kepner's prolific writings is collected in his *Rough News, Daring Views: 1950s' Pioneer Gay Press Journalism* (New York: Harrington Park Press, 1998).

30. Dr. Blanche M. Baker (died 1960), a San Francisco-based psychiatrist, was one of the early professional allies of the gay movement. She spoke and wrote frequently on the need for gay men and lesbians to stop being ashamed of their sexual orientation and to strive for personal acceptance. From January 1959 to June 1960 Baker wrote a regular column for *ONE Magazine* entitled "Toward Understanding." See Blanche M. Baker, "Toward Understanding," *ONE Magazine*, January 1959, pp. 25-27; and John D'Emilio, *Sexual Politics, Sexual Communities: The Making of a Homosexual Minority in the United States, 1940-1970* (Chicago: University of Chicago Press, 1983), p. 117.

31. Dr. Evelyn Hooker (1907-1996) was a professor of psychology at UCLA. In 1954 she began a serious comparative psychological study of gay and heterosexual men, later presenting research-based papers rejecting the prevailing orthodoxy that homosexuality was psychopathological. For example, her paper "The Adjustment of the Male Overt Homosexual," presented before a meeting of the American Psychological Association in 1956, declared that gay men could be as well adjusted psychologically as heterosexual men, and that there was no measurable difference between the two groups of men in her study. Hooker's work was controversial and widely publicized, and was influential in leading to the eventual removal of homosexuality from the American Psychiatric Association's *Diagnostic and Statistical Manual of Psychiatric Disorders* in December 1973. See David W. Dunlap, "Evelyn Hooker, 89, Is Dead: Recast the View of Gay Men," *New York Times*, late ed., 22 November 1996, p. D19; and "The Psychologist — Dr. Evelyn Hooker," in Marcus, *Making History*, pp. 16-25. Dr. Hooker was the subject of the documentary "Changing Our Minds: The Story of Dr. Evelyn Hooker," directed by Richard Schmiechen and produced by David Haugland (West Hollywood, Ca.: Intrepid Productions, 1992).

32. Rt. Rev. Angus J. MacQueen, "Dare to Be Different" ("The Church and You" column), *Toronto Daily Star*, night ed., 6 June 1959, p. 13. Angus MacQueen (1912-) was Moderator of the United Church of Canada from 1958 to 1960. See Angus James MacQueen, *Memory Is My Diary*, 2 vols. (Hantsport, N.S.: Lancelot Press, 1990-91).

33. During his lifetime Bishop (later Archbishop) Fulton J. Sheen (1895-1979) was one of the most prominent spokesmen for the Roman Catholic Church

in America. From 1930 he was a radio preacher, later moving to newspaper columns and television. In 1940 Sheen conducted the first religious service to be telecast. From 1951 to 1957 he was the host of the weekly ABC television series "Life Is Worth Living." See George Dugan, "Archbishop Sheen, Who Preached to Millions Over TV, Is Dead at 84," *New York Times*, late city ed., 10 December 1979, pp. A1, D13; and Fulton J. Sheen, *Treasure in Clay: The Autobiography of Fulton J. Sheen* (Garden City, N.Y.: Doubleday, 1980).

Chapter Five: Gay Personalities of Old Toronto

1. I have been unable to locate George Hislop's letter to Jim Egan and the tape or a transcript of it, although Hislop donated the tape to the Canadian Lesbian and Gay Archives many years ago.

2. For more information on CHAT, see McLeod, *Lesbian and Gay Liberation in Canada*, pp. 59-61.

3. Jimmy Roulston's performances at the Chez Paree before an audience of "'sa-wish' kids" were sometimes mentioned in the tabloids. See, for example, "Toronto's Breeze Around" (column), *Hush Free Press*, 9 October 1948, p. 7.

4. "In 2,000 War Shows, 'Scotty' Wilson Dies," *Toronto Daily Star*, night ed., 25 March 1959, p. 3.

5. "Life Term in Prison Imposed in Stabbing: Murder Charge Reduced," *Globe and Mail*, final ed., 24 September 1960, p. 4; "Lowdown" (column), *Justice Weekly*, 22 October 1960, p. 13; "Salesman Admits Slaying," *Toronto Daily Star*, metro ed., 22 September 1960, p. 65; and "Stabbing Murder Charged," *Toronto Daily Star*, metro ed., 4 May 1960, p. 1.

Chapter Six: Explorations of Gay Male Community in Toronto in the Early 1960s

1. Sidney Katz was one of Canada's most distinguished journalists of the 1950s and 1960s. Much of his work concentrated on medicine and on contemporary social issues, and he was known to take risks. For example, Katz was the first journalist ever to take LSD and describe the experience for a mainstream magazine. See Sidney Katz, "My 12 Hours As a Madman," *Maclean's*, 1 October 1953, pp. 9-13, 46-50, 52-53, 55.

2. Albert Warson, "Blames Lack of Public Disgust for Growth of Homosexuality: Degenerates Parade, Inspector Says," *Globe and Mail*, final ed., 14 November 1963, p. 13. See also Nathan Cohen, "Monday Miscellany" (column), *Toronto Daily Star*, night ed., 13 January 1964, p. 18; and Egan's response, "Police Concern for Homosexual Clubs 'Illogical'" (letter), *Toronto Daily Star*, night ed., 21 January 1964, p. 6.

3. Sidney Katz, "The Homosexual Next Door: A Sober Appraisal of a New Social Phenomenon," *Maclean's*, 22 February 1964, pp. 10-11, 28-30; Sidney

Katz, "The Harsh Facts of Life in the 'Gay' World," *Maclean's*, 7 March 1964, pp. 18, 34-38. See also Gary Kinsman's discussion of this series in his *The Regulation of Desire*, 2nd ed., rev., pp. 251-52.

4. For example: Anonymous, letter, *Maclean's*, 2 May 1964, p. 36; Gordon K. Johnson, "Treating the Homosexual" (letter), *Maclean's*, 2 May 1964, pp. 7, 36; and Louis Stoetzer, letter, *Maclean's*, 2 May 1964, p. 36. Katz's articles also received favourable comment in *ONE Magazine*. See "Tangents: News & Views," *ONE Magazine*, April 1964, p. 18; and Mr. M.J.M., Letter, *ONE Magazine*, June 1964, p. 29.

5. Katz and Egan were scheduled to film an interview for "The Pierre Berton Show" on 20 February 1964, but the segment was cancelled. See Sidney Katz's letter to Jim Egan, 14 February 1964, James Egan Papers, accession 88-006, Canadian Lesbian and Gay Archives, Toronto.

6. [Ron Poulton], "Society and the Homosexual" (part 1), *Toronto Telegram*, final ed., 11 April 1964, p. 7; [Ron Poulton], "The Sick Life" (part 2), *Toronto Telegram*, final ed., 14 April 1964, p. 7; and [Ron Poulton], "Church and Law" (part 3), *Toronto Telegram*, final ed., 15 April 1964, p. 7. Egan's response to these articles was never published in the *Telegram*, but did appear in *Two*. See Jim Egan, "*Two* Guest Editorial," *Two*, no. 2 (1964), pp. 13-19.

7. For a description of the Music Room see Peter Alann, "Very Much Out ... and About: Music Room Private Members Club," *Two*, no. 3 (1964), pp. 23-24; George Graham, "Strange Life of the Gay Ones Behind This Door," *Toronto Telegram*, night five star ed., 7 June 1963, pp. 1-2; and references to "The Club" in Sidney Katz, "The Homosexual Next Door: A Sober Appraisal of a New Social Phenomenon," *Maclean's*, 22 February 1964, pp. 10-11, 28-30.

8. Formal meetings and discussions were held later at the Music Room's sister club, the Melody Room, located at 457 Church Street and active from 1964 to 1966. See, for example, an account of a discussion of homosexuality and religion with a Baptist minister, held at the Melody Room in early 1966: Untitled article, *Two*, no. 9 (1966), p. 28.

9. Dr. William Hogg's identity is somewhat mysterious. I have been unable to confirm that Dr. Hogg worked at the Forensic Clinic in Toronto. However, files at the University of Toronto Archives confirm that William F. Hogg, M.D., a graduate of the University of Western Ontario, was appointed a fellow of the department of psychiatry at the University of Toronto in 1960, and that his employment ceased there in 1961. *Might's Greater Toronto City Directory* lists a Dr. William F. Hogg beginning in 1963, employed as a psychiatrist at the University of Toronto (1963, 1965, 1966), and as a psychiatrist with the Board of Education (1964). I have been unable to locate Dr. Hogg after 1966.

10. It is ironic that Jim and Jack left Toronto in 1964, a year in which several

milestones occurred in the development of a visible local gay community. For example, the first issue of *Gay* (later *Gay International*) was published on 30 March 1964. Although it ceased after only fifteen issues, *Gay* was an important first step in publishing a general interest tabloid for homosexuals. It was also one of the earliest gay publications to use the word "gay" in its title. On 13 April 1964, in Toronto, the Roman Sauna Baths opened at 740 Bay Street. In its day it was one of the largest and most modern gay bathhouses in Canada. In July 1964, *Two* magazine began publication, listing the Melody Room as its editorial office (Egan contributed to *Two*). *Two*'s stated purpose was "to promote knowledge and understanding of the homosexual viewpoint among the general public and to educate homosexuals as to their responsibilities as variants from the current moral and social standards." Finally, on 24 July 1964 Sidney Katz wrote in the *Toronto Daily Star* that plans were being made to form a Homophile Reform Society that would work towards amendments to the Criminal Code (Sidney Katz, "Homosexuals Plan Own Organization," *Toronto Daily Star*, night ed., 25 July 1964, p. 2). For more information on gay organizing in Toronto (and elsewhere in Canada) at this time see McLeod, *Lesbian and Gay Liberation in Canada*.

Afterword

1. Articles and correspondence relating to Jim Egan's activities after he and Jack moved to British Columbia are located in the James Egan Papers, accession 96-130, Canadian Lesbian and Gay Archives, Toronto.

2. Justice Leonard Martin, Reasons for Judgment, *James Egan and John Norris Nesbit v. Her Majesty the Queen in Right of Canada*, Federal Court of Canada, T-2425-88, 2 December 1991, pp. 13-14. See also Stewart Bell, "Gay Couple Not Spousal, Judge Says," *Vancouver Sun*, 5 December 1991, p. B1; Steve Bridger, "B.C. Judge in Egan Case Says Only Traditional Families Are 'Building Blocks of Society,'" *Angles*, February 1992, p. 5; Stephen Brunt, "Homosexual Couple to Sue Over Benefits," *Globe and Mail*, metro ed., 27 August 1988, p. A12; Gabriella Goliger, "Gay Couple Seeks Pension Benefit: B.C. Man Wants Federal Spouse Supplement for His Lover," *XS: A Supplement to Xtra! Magazine*, no. 4 (February 1990), pp. 1, 3; Lora Grindlay, "Spousal Benefits Denied to Gay Couple: Court Ruling Sparks Outrage and a Vow to Keep Fighting," *Vancouver Province*, 5 December 1991, p. A5; John Hanley, "An Unhappy Gay Couple: Old Age Security Act Survives a Challenge from Homosexuals," *British Columbia Report*, 23 December 1991, p. 23; Harry Hill, "Challenging the Charter: Two Gay Men File Suit to Overturn Government Policy that Discriminates against Same-Sex Couples," *Angles*, October 1988, pp. 12-13; and David Vienneau, "Gay Couple Lose Court Bid for Pension," *Toronto Star*, metro ed., 5 December 1991, p. A13.

3. Justices Robertson and Mahoney held the majority view. See J. Bowman, "Gay Case Headed for Canada's Top Court," *North Island News*, 24 October 1993, p. 2; "B.C. Couple Loses Old-Age Pension Appeal," *Vancouver Sun*, 30

April 1993, p. A10; "Federal Court Denies Same-Sex Partner's Benefit Claim — Appeal Underway," Charter Cases/Human Rights Reporter section of *Lancaster Labour Law Reports* 9 (November 1993): 1-3; and Debra M. McAllister, "*Egan*: A Crucible for Human Rights," *National Journal of Constitutional Law* 5 (November 1994): 95-108.

4. *Egan v. Canada* (1995), 124 D.L.R. (4th) 609, [1995] 2 S.C.R. 513. Justices Cory, L'Heureux-Dubé, Iacobucci, McLachlin, and Sopinka ruled that the definition of "spouse" in the Old Age Security Act was discriminatory; Chief Justice Lamer and Justices La Forest, Gonthier, and Major voted no. However, Chief Justice Lamer and Justices La Forest, Gonthier, Major, and Sopinka ruled that the discrimination was justified in this case under section 1 of the Charter; Justices Cory, L'Heureux-Dubé, Iacobucci, and McLachlin voted no.

Much has been written about *Egan v. Canada*. The case is well documented in Casswell, *Lesbians, Gay Men, and Canadian Law*, pp. 371-411, and in Robert Wintemute, "Discrimination against Same-Sex Couples: Sections 15(1) and 1 of the *Charter*: *Egan v. Canada*," *Canadian Bar Review* 74 (December 1995): 682-713. Selected articles from mainstream and gay sources include: Brad Berg, "Fumbling towards Equality: Promise and Peril in *Egan*," *National Journal of Constitutional Law* 5 (June 1995): 263-78; Sean Fine, "Top Court Ponders Spousal Benefits: Gay Couple Argues Discrimination," *Globe and Mail*, metro ed., 2 November 1994, p. A6; Sean Fine and Margaret Philp, "Divorced Mothers, Gay Couples Lose in Court," *Globe and Mail*, metro ed., 26 May 1995, pp. A1, A9; Christopher Guly, "Court Challenge Could Pave the Way to Equality: Longterm Canadian Couple Who Defied the Odds Are Hoping for a Little More Luck," *Washington Blade*, 16 December 1994, p. 14; Neal Hall, "Gay Couple Lose 8-Year Fight for Pension Benefits: Supreme Court Ruling," *Vancouver Sun*, final ed., 26 May 1995, p. A3; Philip Hannan, "Checkered Victory: No Pension for Spouse of 47 Years, Court Rules," *Xtra!*, no. 277 (9 June 1995), pp. 1, 12; Wendy McLellan, "One Battle Is Lost — Another Won," *Vancouver Province*, 26 May 1995, p. A6; Bruce Ryder, "*Egan v. Canada*: Equality Deferred, Again," *Canadian Labour & Employment Law Journal* 4 (1996): 101-110; "Two Decisions on Equality" (editorial), *Globe and Mail*, metro ed., 26 May 1995, p. A14; and David Vienneau, "Fighting the System: Together 46 Years, Gay Couple Take Battle for Benefits to the High Court," *Toronto Star*, metro ed., 23 October 1994, p. A2.

5. Equality for Gays and Lesbians Everywhere (EGALE), "EGALE Responds to *Egan*: 'A Loss But Not a Defeat,'" press release, 25 May 1995, p. 1. Subsequent litigation, such as *Rosenberg v. Canada*, concerning same-sex spousal access to survivors' pension benefits, and *M. v. H.*, a case currently before the Supreme Court involving a lesbian relationship in which one partner is seeking the right to claim spousal support from the other, obviously supports this remark. See Laura Eggertson, "Gays, Lesbians Hail Decision on Pensions: Federal Move Will Lead to Revisions, Activists Say,"

Toronto Star, metro ed., 23 June 1998, pp. A1, A24; and Pam MacEachern, "*Rosenberg v. Canada*: The Impact of *Egan v. Canada* on Lesbian and Gay Equality Claims," *Canadian Labour & Employment Law Journal* 4 (1996): 87-100.

Appendix A: A Chronology of the Life of Jim Egan

1921   James Leo (Jim) Egan was born in Toronto, 14 September, to James Egan and Nellie (Josephine) Engle. The Egan family lived at 281½ George Street at that time.

1922   Charles Egan, Jim's only sibling, was born 14 November.

1924   The Egan family moved to 39 Westlake Avenue.

1927   Jim Egan began school at Holy Name School, 690 Carlaw Avenue, which was operated by the Sisters of St. Joseph.

         John (Jack) Norris Nesbit was born 27 June in Toronto, the son of William S. and Agnes Nesbit.

1930   The Egan family moved to 245 Bain Avenue. [Jim Egan lived there until 1937.]

1934   At the age of thirteen Egan came to realize that he was sexually attracted to males.

1935   By the age of fourteen Jim Egan had become an avid reader, a trait that would continue throughout his life.

1936   James Egan died on 8 January, aged seventy.

ca. 1936   Jim Egan entered the Eastern High School of Commerce, 16 Phin Avenue, taking a mixed science course of biology, chemistry, and physics, as well as English literature and composition. He failed the first year and attended only two months of a second year before abandoning formal schooling.

1937-39   Egan visited his uncle Wilbur Jewison at Bailieboro, Ontario, and worked on farms in the area. After the declaration of war in September 1939, Egan tried to enlist but was rejected due to a corneal scar.

1939-43   Biology always greatly interested Egan, and he spent many hours studying the subject. Late in 1939 he was hired as a departmental technician in the Department of Zoology at the University of Toronto. He later worked at Connaught Laboratories in the insulin production department, and in the tissue culture lab, doing work on typhus, polio, and cancer research under Dr. Raymond Parker.

1943-47   Jim Egan enlisted in the merchant navy and served as an ordinary seaman through the end of the war. He served on several ships, including one year and two months on the *Konge Sverre*, a Norwegian vessel under British registry, and on the *Juan N. Seguine*, a U.S. Liberty Ship. Egan travelled throughout the Mediterranean and served in the South Seas. During and after the war, he came into contact for the first time with a "gay world" while visiting cities like London and Hamburg.

late 1947   Jim Egan quit the merchant navy and returned to Toronto. He soon started going to the Savarin Hotel's beverage room, located at 336-44 Bay Street, which was frequented by gay men. This was the first time Egan realized that there was a community of gay men in Toronto.

Egan discovered that his younger brother, Charles, was gay when he spotted him at the Savarin, sitting at a table of obviously gay men. The brothers never discussed their gay orientation, but it was gradually accepted between them.

1948   In August Jim Egan met Jack Nesbit, first at the Savarin and later at the King Cole Room at the Park Plaza Hotel, located at Bloor Street and Avenue Road. They entered into a relationship, and Jim was soon living with Jack and his parents at 164 Cumberland Street. On 23 August 1948, Jim and Jack exchanged rings and agreed to commit themselves to each other.

1949   By mid year Egan began writing letters to the editor in response to sensational or misleading reports on homosexuality published in mainstream local newspapers such as the *Globe and Mail*, the *Toronto Daily Star*, and the *Toronto Telegram*. None of these early letters was published.

Jim and Jack moved to Oak Ridges, about fifteen miles north of Toronto, late in the year. There they operated a biological supply business and established their first home together.

1950   Throughout 1950 Egan sent letters to mainstream American magazines such as *Coronet*, *The Ladies' Home Journal*, *Parents' Magazine*, and *Redbook Magazine*, trying to sell story ideas that depicted homosexuality in an honest and straightforward fashion. His ideas were rejected.

Egan's earliest known publications appeared on 16 May; a letter signed J.L.E. in *Flash*, and a letter defending the Kinsey Report, signed James Egan, in the *Globe and Mail*. Soon, his letters appeared regularly in the Toronto tabloids, such as *Flash*, *Justice Weekly*, and *True News Times (TNT)*.

In September Egan decided to write a book detailing the social and legal situation of homosexuals in various countries of the world. Over the next two months he wrote a letter of inquiry to every foreign embassy in Ottawa, requesting a copy of the country's penal code and information about homosexuality and the law. Many of the legations responded. Egan's project was abandoned when Donald Webster Cory (pseud.) published his work *The Homosexual in America: A Subjective Approach* (New York, 1951).

"I Am a Homosexual," by Leo Engle (pseud., the name of Egan's maternal grandfather), a long essay sympathetic to homosexuality, was published in the December 1950 issue of the American men's magazine *Sir!*. Egan received letters from several readers, and began a lengthy correspondence with at least two of them.

1951   In January Egan began corresponding with the early American homophile activist Henry Gerber. Their correspondence extended into May 1951.

Egan's seven-part series "Aspects of Homosexuality" appeared weekly in *True News Times (TNT)*, beginning on 19 November and extending to 31 December.

1953   Egan began to correspond with members of the Mattachine Society in Los Angeles.

1953-54 "Homosexual Concepts," a twelve-part series by Egan, was published in *Justice Weekly* between 5 December 1953 and 27 February 1954. This was followed by another, untitled series, published in fifteen parts between 6 March and 12 June 1954.

1955   Jim and Jack sold the property at Oak Ridges and purchased a farm near Chesley, Ontario, where they grew malting barley and raised pigs and turkeys.

On 19 March *Justice Weekly* published a brief that Egan had sent to the Parliamentary Legislative Committee of the House of Commons concerning proposed amendments to Section 206 of the Canadian Criminal Code, regarding gross indecency.

1958   Egan and Nesbit decided to abandon farming and moved to Beamsville, Ontario, where they established The Nature Shop, a pet and garden supply store, as well as a small wholesale biological supply company.

1959   Jim and Jack attended the fifth Midwinter Institute of ONE, Incorporated, in Los Angeles, from 30 January through 1 February. They met many leading homophile activists during this conference, including Dr. Blanche Baker, Dr. Evelyn Hooker, Jim Kepner, and W. Dorr Legg. Egan was inspired by these contacts to write articles for ONE Magazine; two articles were published in October and December.

Throughout the year Egan wrote letters relating to gay topics, some of which were published in Look, Saturday Night, the Toronto Daily Star, and other magazines and newspapers.

1960   In May Jim's friend Alex Bakalis was murdered by a young male hustler. Egan followed the case closely, and attended the preliminary hearing.

1963   Egan and Nesbit moved to Toronto late in the year and lived at 1052A Bloor Street West.

1964   Sidney Katz's two-part series "The Homosexual Next Door: A Sober Appraisal of a New Social Phenomenon" was published in Maclean's magazine during February-March. These are considered to be the first full-scale articles published in a mainstream Canadian publication to take a generally positive view of homosexuality. Katz used Egan (and Jim's extensive library) as sources of information about homosexuality, and relied on Egan to provide a practical tour of local gay sites.

Early in the year Jim and Jack's relationship came under pressure due to Jack's increasingly public gay activism. The couple decided to part company; the separation lasted several months. During this time Egan started another biological specimen business and spent many evenings at the Music Room, one of Toronto's first gay clubs.

From the spring until June, Egan met weekly with about six other gay men for informal discussions concerning gay life. These sessions were attended by Dr. William Hogg, a psychiatrist, who acted as observer.

By June Egan and Nesbit were reunited. Egan decided to abandon gay activism in favour of his relationship with Jack, and they decided to move away from Toronto. They loaded all of their belongings into a five-ton truck and drove across Canada to British Columbia, where they intended to begin a new life together.

In July Egan and Nesbit settled in Duncan, B.C., where they established the Jamack Biological Supply Company, specializing in marine specimens. In Duncan, Jim developed a great interest in the environmental movement and joined the Society for the Prevention of Environmental Collapse (SPEC).

1968   Jim and Jack moved to Thetis Island, where they purchased a property on Telegraph Harbour and continued their thriving business.

1972   Egan and Nesbit decided to retire from their business, sold the property on Thetis Island, and moved to Chemainus, B.C., where they lived in a rented cabin. At Chemainus Jim was involved in environmental work.

1974   The couple bought a property at Merville, B.C., on which they built a large stackwall house. Jack began to work at the local crisis centre, while Jim continued his environmental work.

1980   Egan joined the Save Our Straits Committee to block a plan to allow the pumping of untreated sewage into the Strait of Georgia. The committee was successful.

1981   Egan was elected as a regional director for Electoral Area B of the Regional District of Comox-Strathcona. He was the first openly gay man living in an openly gay relationship to be elected to public office in Canada. Egan was re-elected twice and served from 1981 until 1993, when he decided not to stand for re-election.

1985   Egan and Nesbit moved to a bungalow on the outskirts of Courtenay, B.C. They started to meet local gay people, and in the fall started the Comox Valley branch of the Island Gay Society. They sponsored a drop-in at their home once a month; the drop-in lasted for eleven years, until 1996.

1986   "A Perfect Beginner: Jim Egan and the Tabloids," by Alfred Taylor (pseud. of Philip McLeod), was published in the September issue of the *Canadian Lesbian and Gay History Network Newsletter*.

Robert Champagne's interview of Egan, "Canada's Pioneer Gay Activist: Jim Egan," was published in the December-January 1986-87 issue of *Rites*.

1987   On 25 February Jim and Jack applied on Jack's behalf for the spousal allowance benefit provided under the Old Age Security Act. Health and Welfare Canada's denial of the benefit one week later set the stage for a court challenge test case under the Canadian Charter of Rights and Freedoms.

Jim Egan: Canada's Pioneer Gay Activist, compiled and introduced by Robert Champagne, was published by the Canadian Lesbian and Gay History Network.

1988   On 6 December Egan and Nesbit brought an action in the Trial Division of the Federal Court of Canada claiming discrimination under the Old Age Security Act in its definition of "spouse." They claimed the current definition was unconstitutional in that it discriminated against same-sex couples on the basis of gender and sexual orientation, contrary to section 15(1) of the Charter.

1991   On 2 December Justice Leonard Martin dismissed the action, declaring that their relationship was "not a spousal one."

1992   On 12 August Egan and Nesbit appealed the ruling in the Federal Court of Appeal, focussing on whether the restrictive definition of "spouse" in the Old Age Security Act violated section 15(1) of the Charter on the basis of discrimination based on sexual orientation.

1993   The Federal Court of Appeal upheld the decision of the lower court, ruling on 29 April that Egan and Nesbit had not been discriminated against because of their sexual orientation. On 2 June, Egan and Nesbit filed an application to appeal to the Supreme Court of Canada.

1994   Egan served as president of the North Island AIDS Coalition.

        Egan and Nesbit's appeal was heard in the Supreme Court on 1 November.

1995   On 25 May the Supreme Court of Canada rendered its decision in the case of *Egan and Nesbit v. Canada*; the appeal was dismissed. The justices ruled that "sexual orientation" must be read into the Charter as a ground of discrimination; they also ruled that discrimination was justified in this case under section 1 of the Charter.

        Egan was presented with a national human rights award by the Lambda Foundation for Excellence on 28 May in Ottawa.

        Egan and Nesbit were the honorary grand marshals at both the Toronto and Vancouver Pride celebrations.

1996   Egan addressed a conference of Canadian human rights commissioners on 2 June in Victoria, sponsored by the British Columbia Human Rights Commission.

        David Adkin's documentary "Jim Loves Jack: The James Egan Story" was released.

Egan and Nesbit were one of the couples featured in Michael Riordon's book *Out Our Way: Gay and Lesbian Life in the Country.*

1997   In recognition of his community service, Egan was presented with a Paul Harris Fellowship by Rotary International in September.

1998   Egan addressed a plenary session entitled "Not a Faggoty Dress-up Party: Disrobing the Supreme Court of Canada in the Post-Egan Era" at the conference Queering the Nation, held at York University on 27 June.

On 23 August, Jim Egan and Jack Nesbit celebrated the fiftieth anniversary of their relationship.

Appendix B: A Checklist of Publications by Jim Egan, 1950-1964

This checklist is based upon materials in the James Egan Papers (accessions 88-006 and 96-130) at the Canadian Lesbian and Gay Archives, Toronto. Although Egan was generally careful in keeping a scrapbook of his publications, unfortunately he was unable to know if all of the letters he sent to newspapers and magazines were published. As a result, his collection of clippings is incomplete. I have undertaken additional research to locate fugitive publications and have attempted to examine each item personally. However, I have been unable to locate extensive archival collections for most of the Toronto tabloids of this period, including *Flash*, *The Rocket*, *Tab*, and *True News Times (TNT)*. I have therefore been unable to undertake a comprehensive examination of these titles for additional items, and could not verify page numbers for several clippings in Egan's papers. Unknown page numbers are indicated in the citations by "p. ?" I have examined the substantial collections of *Hush Free Press* and *Justice Weekly* at the Baldwin Room, Toronto Reference Library. The many entries in this checklist marked "JECPGA" are easily accessible, however, as they are reproduced in facsimile in *Jim Egan: Canada's Pioneer Gay Activist*, compiled and introduced by Robert Champagne (Toronto: Canadian Lesbian and Gay History Network, 1987).

1950

J.L.E., "Reader Defends Homos Says They're Inverts" (letter), *Flash*, 16 May 1950, pp. 16, 19. JECPGA, p. 9

James Egan, "Views Vary on New Kinsey Report: For Publication" (letter), *Globe and Mail*, final ed., 16 May 1950, p. 6. JECPGA, p. 10.

J.L.E., "Homos Acts Not Concern of Outsiders Says One" (letter), *Flash*, 13 June 1950, p. 12. JECPGA, p. 11.

J.L.E., Letter, *Flash*, [1950, after 27 June], p. ?. JECPGA, p. 12.

J.L.E., "TNT Taken to Task by ????" (letter), *True News Times (TNT)*, 16 October 1950, p. 11. JECPGA, p. 14.

J.L.E., Letter, *True News Times (TNT)*, 30 October 1950, p. ?. JECPGA, p. 15.

Leo Engle (pseud.), "I Am a Homosexual," *Sir!*, December 1950, pp. ?.

[late 1950, before 16 January 1951.] Advertisement in *Writer's Digest* [see Henry Gerber's letter to Jim Egan, 16 January 1951.]

1951

J.L.E., "Fairy Nice" (letter), *True News Times (TNT)*, 19 February 1951, p. ?. JECPGA, p. 18.

J.L.E., Letter, *Flash*, 26 March 1951, p. ?. JECPGA, p. 18.

J.L.E., Letter, *Flash*, [16 April 1951?], p. ?.

J.L.E., "Should Abolish Absurd Anti-Homosexual Laws, Asserts Correspondent" (letter), *Justice Weekly*, 19 May 1951, p. 9. JECPGA, p. 20.

J.L.E., Letter, *Flash*, 18 June 1951, p. ?. JECPGA, p. 21.

J.L.E., "Reader Claims Abolition of Anti-Homosexual Laws Would Lessen Sex Crimes" (letter), *Justice Weekly*, 28 July 1951, pp. 15, 16. JECPGA, p. 23.

J.L.E., Letter, *True News Times (TNT)*, 12 November 1951, p. ?. JECPGA, p. 25.

[Unsigned], "Aspects of Homosexuality: History and Background Ancient Widespread in Land of Pharohs [sic]" (series, part one), *True News Times (TNT)*, 19 November 1951, pp. 5, 12. JECPGA, pp. 26-27.

[Unsigned], "Aspects of Homosexuality: Discussion of the Legal Aspects in the Life of a Homosexual" (series, part two), *True News Times (TNT)*, 26 November 1951, pp. 5, 14. JECPGA, pp. 28-29.

[Unsigned], "Aspects of Homosexuality: Discussion of the Legal Aspects in the Life of a Homosexual" (series, part three), *True News Times (TNT)*, 3 December 1951, pp. 5, 14. JECPGA, pp. 30-31.

[Unsigned], "Aspects of Homosexuality: Discussion of Scientific Approach to This Most Baffling Question" (series, part four), *True News Times (TNT)*, 10 December 1951, pp. 5, 14. JECPGA, pp. 32-33.

[Unsigned], "Aspects of Homosexuality: Discussion of Scientific Approach to This Most Baffling Question" (series, part five), *True News Times (TNT)*, 17 December 1951, pp. 5, 14. JECPGA, pp. 34-35.

[Unsigned], "Homosexual 'Marriages' Just Like Normal: Feminine Types Not Typical Homo Many Quiet and Not Indiscreet Many 'Happy Marriages' Last" (series, part six), *True News Times (TNT)*, 24 December 1951, pp. 5, 14. JECPGA, pp. 36-37.

[Unsigned], "More Tolerance Needed Toward Homos: Homosexuals 'Fall Guys' for Pressure Groups and Governments — Need to Be Properly Understood" (series, part seven), *True News Times (TNT)*, 31 December 1951, pp. 5, 11. JECPGA, pp. 38-39.

1952

J.L.E., Letter, *Front Page*, [March 1952?], p. ?.

J.L.E., Letter, *Justice Weekly*, 3 May 1952, pp. 11, 16. JECPGA, p. 41.

J.L.E., Letter, *Justice Weekly*, 31 May 1952, p. 5. JECPGA, p. 41.

1953

J.L.E., "Treatment of Homosexuals Is Recommended by Reader Who Finds Fault With Law" (letter), *Justice Weekly*, 21 February 1953, p. 16. JECPGA, p. 42.

J.L.E., Letter, *Justice Weekly*, 14 March 1953, p. 14. JECPGA, p. 43.

J.L.E., Letter, *Flash*, 11 July 1953, p. ?. JECPGA, p. 43.

J.L.E., Letter, *Flash*, 5 September 1953, p. ?. JECPGA, p. 43.

J.L.E., "How To Deal With Homosexuals Told By Authority on Subject" (letter), *Justice Weekly*, 21 November 1953, pp. 12, 16. JECPGA, p. 45.

[Unsigned], "Series of Articles on Homosexuality and Homosexuals Begins Next Week: Purpose to Bring About a Better Understanding Between Hetero and Homo," *Justice Weekly*, 28 November 1953, p. 12. JECPGA, p. 47.

J.L.E., "Grave Injustice" (letter), *Toronto Telegram*, blue streak metropolitan ed., 30 November 1953, p. 6. JECPGA, p. 47.

J.L.E., "Homosexual Concepts" (column), *Justice Weekly*, 5 December 1953, p. 13. JECPGA, p. 48.

J.L.E., "Homosexual Concepts: The Mattachine Society" (column), *Justice Weekly*, 12 December 1953, p. 13. JECPGA, p. 49.

J.L.E., "Homosexual Concepts" (column), *Justice Weekly*, 19 December 1953, p. 13. JECPGA, p. 50.

J.L.E., "Homosexual Concepts" (column), *Justice Weekly*, 26 December 1953, p. 13. JECPGA, p. 52.

1954

J.L.E., "Homosexual Concepts" (column), *Justice Weekly*, 2 January 1954, p. 13. JECPGA, p. 54.

J.L.E., "Homosexual Concepts" (column), *Justice Weekly*, 9 January 1954, p. 13. JECPGA, p. 55.

J.L.E., "Homosexual Concepts" (column), *Justice Weekly*, 16 January 1954, p. 13. JECPGA, p. 56.

J.L.E., "Homosexual Concepts" (column), *Justice Weekly*, 23 January 1954, p. 13. JECPGA, p. 57.

J.L.E., "Homosexual Concepts" (column), *Justice Weekly*, 30 January 1954, p. 13. JECPGA, p. 58.

J.L.E., "Homosexual Concepts" (column), *Justice Weekly*, 13 February 1954, p. 13. JECPGA, p. 59.

J.L.E., "Homosexual Concepts" (column), *Justice Weekly*, 20 February 1954, pp. 13, 15. JECPGA, p. 60.

J.L.E., "Homosexual Concepts" (column), *Justice Weekly*, 27 February 1954, p. 13. JECPGA, p. 61.

J.L.E., "Widespread Nature of Homosexuality Revealed in Kinsey Report on Male's Sexual Behaviour" (series, part one), *Justice Weekly*, 6 March 1954, p. 13. JECPGA, p. 62.

J.L.E., "Most Fantastic Witch-Hunt Since Inquisition Was Followed by Dismissal of Homosexuals by the Hundreds from U.S. Government Offices" (series, part two), *Justice Weekly*, 13 March 1954, p. 13. JECPGA, p. 63.

J.L.E., "Anti-Homosexual Legislation Automatically Making Criminals of Them Deeply Resented by Members of One-Time Little Known Group" (series, part three), *Justice Weekly*, 20 March 1954, p. 13. JECPGA, p. 64.

J.L.E., "Rash of Magazine Stories Catapulted Homosexual Minority into Limelight; Effects Far-Reaching and Unforeseen" (series, part four), *Justice Weekly*, 27 March 1954, pp. 13, 16. JECPGA, p. 65.

J.L.E., "Persecution of Homosexuals Gets Blamed for Their Increased Activity in Public" (series, part five), *Justice Weekly*, 3 April 1954, p. 13. JECPGA, p. 66.

J.L.E., "Inability of Investigating Committees to Examine Homosexual's Side of Fence Explains the Failure to Solve Problem" (series, part six), *Justice Weekly*, 10 April 1954, p. 13. JECPGA, p. 67.

J.L.E., "Homosexuals Are Not Perverts Bent on Corruption of Youth, Says Writer" (series, part seven), *Justice Weekly*, 17 April 1954, p. 13. JECPGA, p. 68.

J.L.E., "Two Suggestions Submitted to Cope With the Problem of Homosexuality" (series, part eight), *Justice Weekly*, 24 April 1954, p. 13. JECPGA, p. 69.

J.L.E., "Description 'Gay' Used by Homosexuals No Misnomer, According to This Writer" (series, part nine), *Justice Weekly*, 1 May 1954, p. 13. JECPGA, p. 70.

[Unsigned], "Present Anti-Homosexual Legislation Greatest Bar to Solution of Problem Opinion Held by Articles Writer J.L.E." (series), *Justice Weekly*, 8 May 1954, p. 12. JECPGA, p. 72.

J.L.E., "Cause and Cure of Homosexuality Result in Violent Disagreements Every Time These Questions Asked" (series), *Justice Weekly*, 15 May 1954, p. 12. JECPGA, p. 73.

[Unsigned], "Homosexual Can Lead Happy Life Maintains Articles Writer J.L.E.; Disposes of Fantastic Theories" (series), *Justice Weekly*, 22 May 1954, p. 12. JECPGA, p. 74.

J.L.E., "Writer 'J.L.E.' Debunks Pet Theories Formulated in Recent Years Seeking to Explain Cause of Homosexuality" (series), *Justice Weekly*, 29 May 1954, p. 12. JECPGA, p. 75.

J.L.E., "Validity of the 'Inborn' Theory in Connection with Homosexuals Expounded by 'Justice' Writer" (series), *Justice Weekly*, 5 June 1954, p. 12. JECPGA, p. 76.

J.L.E., "Very Idea of Cure for Homosexuality Ridiculous, Writer's Final Analysis" (series), *Justice Weekly*, 12 June 1954, p. 12. JECPGA, p. 77.

J.L.E., "J.L.E. Answers Letter from Canadian Mother" (letter), *Justice Weekly*, 26 June 1954, pp. 5, 9. JECPGA, p. 79.

1955

[Unsigned], "Parliamentary Legislative Committee Ignored This Letter from Homosexual Suggesting Changes in Criminal Code" (letter), *Justice Weekly*, 19 March 1955, pp. 5, 14. JECPGA, pp. 83-84.

1959

James Egan, "Hitler's World" (letter), *Look*, 17 February 1959, p. 14. JECPGA, p. 86.

James Egan, "Nathan Cohen's Corner: The Readers Have Their Say" (letter), *Toronto Daily Star*, metro ed., 14 March 1959, p. 28. JECPGA, p. 86.

James Egan, "The Basic Bard" (letter), *Saturday Night*, 6 June 1959, p. 3. JECPGA, p. 86.

James Egan, "Nathan Cohen's Corner: Readers Have Their Say" (letter), *Toronto Daily Star*, metro ed., 18 July 1959, p. 25.

James Egan, Letter, *Beamsville Express*, [after 30 July 1959], pp. ?, 3. JECPGA, p. 87.

James Egan, "Roger Casement" (letter), *Toronto Daily Star*, metro ed., 25 August 1959, p. 6. JECPGA, p. 87.

James Egan, "Mailbag" (letter), *Maclean's*, 29 August 1959, p. 4. JECPGA, p. 87.

Jim Egan, "Toronto Fairy-Go-Round," *ONE Magazine*, October 1959, pp. 10-13. Reprinted as "So the Chief of Police Said to the Royal Commission ...: 'Toronto Fairy-Go-Round,'" *Justice Weekly*, 7 November 1959, pp. 5, 15. JECPGA, pp. 88-89.

Jim Egan, "Homosexual Marriage — Fact or Fancy?" *ONE Magazine*, December 1959, pp. 6-9. JECPGA, pp. 90-91. Reprinted in *Justice Weekly*, 23 January 1960, pp. 5, 16.

1960

James Egan, "Apologize to Homos" (letter), *Hush Free Press*, 12 March 1960, p. 11.

James Egan, Letter, *Flash*, 2 April 1960, p. ?.

James Egan, "Guard Rights" (letter), *Toronto Daily Star*, metro ed., 5 April 1960, p. 6. JECPGA, p. 92.

James Egan, "Protests Censor Group Is 'Invasion of Civil Rights'" (letter), *Toronto Daily Star*, metro ed., 26 May 1960, p. 6. JECPGA, p. 92.

Jim Egan, "Readers on Writers" (letter), *ONE Magazine*, June 1960, pp. 6-8.

James Egan, "Canada's 'Vicious' Laws against Homosexuality" (letter), *Toronto Daily Star*, metro ed., 5 July 1960, p. 6. JECPGA, p. 92.

James Egan, "Embarrassing Memory" (letter), *Saturday Night*, 20 August 1960, p. 2. JECPGA, p. 92.

1961

Regular Reader (pseud.), "Letters on Subject of Discipline, the Treatment of

Sexual Deviates and Dressing Young Boys Like Girls" (letter), *Justice Weekly*, 22 July 1961, pp. 10, 12. JECPGA, p. 93.

James Egan, "For Legal Reform" (letter), *Toronto Daily Star*, night ed., 26 July 1961, p. 6. JECPGA, p. 94.

Jim Egan, "Blueprint for Partnership," *ONE Magazine*, November 1961, pp. 20-23.

James Egan, "Unctuous Pundits" (letter), *Toronto Daily Star*, night ed., 13 December 1961, p. 6. JECPGA, p. 94.

1962

James Egan, "More Standards" (letter), *Saturday Night*, 17 March 1962, p. 3. JECPGA, p. 94.

James Egan, "Our Readers Speak — Con" (letter), *Canadian Commentator*, June 1962, p. 15.

1963

James Egan, "Boy, Oh Boy!" (letter), *Saturday Night*, September 1963, p. 8. JECPGA, p. 97.

James Egan, "'No Crime in Private Homosexual Acts between Consenting Adults'" (letter), *Toronto Daily Star*, night ed., 7 September 1963, p. 6. JECPGA, p. 95.

James Egan, Letters to the Editor, *Tab Confidential*, 28 September 1963, pp. 5, 8. JECPGA, p. 97.

James Egan, "Civil Liberties and the Homosexual" ("Against the Grain" column), *Toronto Daily Star*, night ed., 23 October 1963, p. 7. JECPGA, p. 98.

James Egan, "Homosexuals" (letter), *Globe and Mail*, final ed., 23 November 1963, p. 6. JECPGA, p. 101.

1964

Jim Egan, "*Two* Guest Editorial," *Two*, no. 2 (1964), pp. 13-19. JECPGA, pp. 102-105.

James Egan, "Police Concern for Homosexual Clubs 'Illogical'" (letter), *Toronto Daily Star*, night ed., 21 January 1964, p. 6. JECPGA, p. 101.

Appendix C: A Checklist of Publications Concerning or in Reply to Jim Egan, 1950-1964

As with Appendix B, this checklist is based upon materials in the James Egan Papers (accessions 88-006 and 96-130) at the Canadian Lesbian and Gay Archives, Toronto. The collection of clippings there is incomplete, and I have undertaken additional research to locate fugitive publications concerning or in reply to Egan, and have attempted to examine each item personally. As I have been unable to locate extensive archival collections of most of the Toronto tabloids for this period, this checklist contains missing page numbers for some items that are present in Egan's papers. Entries marked "JECPGA" are reproduced in facsimile in *Jim Egan: Canada's Pioneer Gay Activist*, compiled and introduced by Robert Champagne (Toronto: Canadian Lesbian and Gay History Network, 1987).

1950

Percival Prosser, Letter, *Flash*, [May-June 1950?], p. ?.

Oscar, Letter, *Flash*, 23 May 1950, p. ?. JECPGA, p. 10.

Julian Farnley, "Says Homos Are Part of Modern Depravity" (letter), *Flash*, 30 May 1950, p. 16. JECPGA, p. 10.

A.B.C., Letter, *Flash*, 27 June 1950, p. ?.

Julian Farnley, "Inverts Can Control Selves Friend of Many Declares!" (letter), *Flash*, 27 June 1950, p. ?. JECPGA, p. 12.

L.F.I., "Defender of Homos Defended" (letter), *True News Times (TNT)*, 13 November 1950, p. ?. JECPGA, p. 15.

1951

S.L., Letter, *True News Times (TNT)*, [19 February 1951?], p. ?. JECPGA, p. 15.

P.P., Letter, *Flash*, 16 April 1951, p. ?. JECPGA, p. 18.

L.D. Demarest, Letter, *Justice Weekly*, 21 July 1951, p. 15. JECPGA, p. 21.

[Mother Goose], "A Study in Lavender" (gossip column), *True News Times (TNT)*, 13 August 1951, p. 14. JECPGA, p. 25.

[Mother Goose], "A Study in Lavender" (gossip column), *True News Times (TNT)*, 26 November 1951, p. 14.

[Mother Goose], "A Study in Lavender" (gossip column), *True News Times (TNT)*, 31 December 1951, p. 13.

1952

[Mother Goose], "Fairy Tales Are Retold" (gossip column), *The Rocket*, 7 June 1952, p. 12.

1953

Homo, "This Homo Wants No Sympathy" (letter), *Front Page*, [1953?], p. ?.

J.M., "Aid for Two Homosexuals Asked by Alarmed Reader" (letter), *Justice Weekly*, 14 November 1953, p. 3. JECPGA, p. 44.

N.B., "Readers Voice Opinions on Homosexual Articles" (letter), *Justice Weekly*, 19 December 1953, p. 16. JECPGA, p. 51.

Pioneer, "Readers Voice Opinions on Homosexual Articles" (letter), *Justice Weekly*, 19 December 1953, pp. 13, 16. JECPGA, pp. 50-51.

M.J., "Readers Voice Opinions on Homosexual Articles" (letter), *Justice Weekly*, 26 December 1953, p. 13. JECPGA, p. 52.

1954

Cardinal, "Readers Voice Opinions on Homosexual Articles" (letter), *Justice Weekly*, 16 January 1954, p. 14. JECPGA, p. 56.

Homo, "Readers Voice Opinions on Homosexual Articles" (letter), *Justice Weekly*, 16 January 1954, p. 13.

E.C.M., "Readers Voice Opinions on Homosexual Articles" (letter), *Justice Weekly*, 16 January 1954, pp. 13, 14.

W.C.W., "Readers Voice Opinions on Homosexual Articles" (letter), *Justice Weekly*, 30 January 1954, pp. 13, 16. JECPGA, p. 58.

E.B.O., "Readers Voice Opinions on Homosexual Articles" (letter), *Justice Weekly*, 27 February 1954, p. 13. JECPGA, p. 61.

N.B., "Readers Voice Opinions on Homosexual Articles" (letter), *Justice Weekly*, 6 March 1954, p. 13.

Grateful Parent, "Father of Young Homosexual Grateful for Advice Given by 'Justice' Writer" (letter), *Justice Weekly*, 27 March 1954, pp. 13, 16. JECPGA, p. 46.

One of Them, "'One of Them' Insists That Affections between Two of Same Sex as Satisfying and Real as between Two Heterosexuals" (letter), *Justice Weekly*, 1 May 1954, p. 5.

Canadian Mother, "Homos Embarrass Her Says Canadian Mother in Answer to 'J.L.E.'" (letter), *Justice Weekly*, 10 July 1954, p. 9. JECPGA, p. 79.

A.C.B., "Letters to the Editor" (letter), *Justice Weekly*, 14 August 1954, p. 15. JECPGA, p. 81.

Miriam, "Letters to the Editor" (letter), *Justice Weekly*, 14 August 1954, p. 11. JECPGA, p. 80.

Bud S., "Letters to the Editor" (letter), *Justice Weekly*, 14 August 1954, pp. 11, 15. JECPGA, pp. 80-81.

1959

L.V. Scott, "Shakespeare's Virtue" (letter), *Saturday Night*, 4 July 1959, p. 2. JECPGA, p. 86.

1960

Mr. N., "Matters Legal & Otherwise" (letter), *ONE Magazine*, January 1960, p. 32.

Miss V., "Homosexual Marriage" (letter), *ONE Magazine*, March 1960, p. 30.

Mr. C. and Mr. P., "Homosexual Marriage" (letter), *ONE Magazine*, March 1960, p. 30.

Mr. H., "Homosexual Marriage" (letter), *ONE Magazine*, March 1960, p. 30.

Mr. K, "Homosexual Marriage" (letter), *ONE Magazine*, March 1960, p. 30.

M. Wilson, "Reader to Reader" (letter), *Flash*, [after 2 April 1960], p. ?.

Michael, "Open Letter: The Honorable Davie Fulton, Ottawa, Ontario, Canada" (letter), *ONE Magazine*, December 1960, pp. 9-11.

1962

Mr. G., "Comments on Contents" (letter), *ONE Magazine*, March 1962, p. 29.

Mr. W., "Comments on Contents" (letter), *ONE Magazine*, March 1962, p. 29.

1963

Sheila Sword, "Colossal Nerve" (letter), *Toronto Daily Star*, night ed., 10 September 1963, p. 6. JECPGA, p. 95.

H.H., "Sex Plebiscite" (letter), *Toronto Daily Star*, night ed., 12 September 1963, p. 6. JECPGA, p. 95.

Ernest C. Fetzer, "Perverse" (letter), *Toronto Daily Star*, night ed., 13 September 1963, p. 6. JECPGA, p. 95.

Mrs. W. Walsh, "'Homosexuality Aberration: Don't Condone It'" (letter), *Toronto Daily Star*, night ed., 13 September 1963, p. 6. JECPGA, p. 95.

C.M. Dier, "'All of Us Have a Certain Degree of Homosexuality'" (letter), *Toronto Daily Star*, night ed., 17 September 1963, p. 6. JECPGA, p. 96.

Sheila Sword, "Misuse of Sex" (letter), *Toronto Daily Star*, night ed., 17 September 1963, p. 6. JECPGA, p. 96.

Thomas Williams, "License to Lust" (letter), *Toronto Daily Star*, night ed., 17 September 1963, p. 6. JECPGA, p. 96.

S. Adams, "Out of Context" (letter), *Toronto Daily Star*, all star ed., 26 October 1963, p. 6. JECPGA, p. 99.

Christa Hanf, "'Fear of Sex Brands Homosexuals as Menace'" (letter), *Toronto Daily Star*, all star ed., 26 October 1963, p. 6. JECPGA, p. 99.

A Reader, "Above the Law" (letter), *Toronto Daily Star*, all star ed., 26 October 1963, p. 6. JECPGA, p. 99.

Reader, "Run by Rats" (letter), *Toronto Daily Star*, all star ed., 26 October 1963, p. 6. JECPGA, p. 99.

John Smith, "Mental Disease" (letter), *Toronto Daily Star*, all star ed., 26 October 1963, p. 6. JECPGA, p. 99.

Canadiana, "Abomination" (letter), *Toronto Daily Star*, night ed., 30 October 1963, p. 6. JECPGA, p. 99.

John Tasco, "Ignorance" (letter), *Toronto Daily Star*, night ed., 31 October 1963, p. 6. JECPGA, p. 99.

Quo Vadis, "Dare an M.P. Propose Relaxing Laws against Homosexuals?" (letter), *Toronto Daily Star*, night ed., 4 November 1963, p. 6. JECPGA, p. 100.

Joe Tensee, "Joe Tensee's Confidential Diary" (column), *Tab Confidential*, 16 November 1963, p. 12. JECPGA, p. 100.

1964

T.W., "'A Lot of Dirt'" (letter), *Toronto Daily Star*, night ed., 27 January 1964, p. 6. JECPGA, p. 101.

Appendix D: The Correspondence of Jim Egan, 1950-1964

This calendar of correspondence is based on the contents of the James Egan Papers, accessions 88-006 and 96-130, at the Canadian Lesbian and Gay Archives, Toronto. Although Egan kept carbon copies of some of his outgoing correspondence, numerous letters sent by him do not survive in the Egan papers. Egan was much more careful about keeping incoming correspondence, much of which has survived. I have tried to include approximate dates for undated letters, based on any information found in the return or related correspondence.

Correspondence Sent by Jim Egan

1950

[undated, 26 February.] Greenberg Publishers, New York. ms, 2 pp.

6 May. The Editor, *Globe and Mail*, Toronto. ts, 1 p., with ms annotations.

[undated, June?] The Editor, *Sir!*, Volitant Publishing Corporation, New York. ts, 1 p.

[undated, July?] The Editor, *Esquire Magazine*, Chicago. ts, 2 pp.

8 August. William Allison, Articles Editor, *Redbook Magazine*, New York. ts, 1 p.

23 August. Gordon Carroll, Editor, *Coronet Magazine*, New York. ts, 1 p.

21 September. The Editor, *Flash Weekly*, Toronto. ts, 2 pp., with ms annotations.

11 October. The Editor, *Flash Weekly*, Toronto. ts, 1 p., with ms annotations.

24 November. Dr. L.F. Freed, Johannesburg. ts, 1 p.

1951

25 March. The Editor, *Time Magazine*, New York. ts, 1 p.

15 July. The Editor, *Justice Weekly*, Toronto. ts, 2 pp., with additional 5 pp. of ts drafts attached.

1952

7 August. James Bannerman, C.B.C. Studios, Toronto. ts, 1 p. [Two versions, drafts?]

1953

[undated, late March.] An article, "The Homosexual Problem Can Be Solved," sent to Joseph Corona, Editor, *Adam — A Man's Magazine*, New York. ts, 13 pp. [The manuscript, but not the covering letter, survives in Egan's papers; see also Corona's reply of 8 April 1953.]

25 June. Noah Sarlat, New York. ts, 1 p., returned to Egan with a brief, undated annotation by Sarlat.

4 November. Dr. Frank Caprio, c/o Linacre Press, Inc., Washington, D.C. ts, 6 pp. [incomplete].

16 November. The Editor, *Evening Telegram*, Toronto. ts, 1 p.

[undated, late November.] Mr. J.M., c/o *Justice Weekly*, Toronto. ts, 3 pp.

[undated, December?] ONE, Incorporated, Los Angeles. ts, 1 p.

1954

29 January. Roy Ald, Associate Editor, *True Confessions*, New York. ts, 3 pp., with attached 3 pp. revised draft.

[undated, 12 March.] Salter Hayden, Q.C.; Don Brown, Q.C., Members of the Parliamentary Legislative Committee [Joint Committee of the Senate and the House of Commons Dealing with Capital and Corporal Punishment and Lotteries], House of Commons, Ottawa. ts, 3 pp., with two separate 3 pp. ts drafts attached.

20 April. The Editor, *Toronto Daily Star*. ts, 1 p.

1955

15 April. Parent's Action League, Toronto. ts, 1 p.

1959

21 May. The Editor, *Toronto Daily Star*. ts, 1 p., with annotations.

8 June. Rt. Rev. A.J. MacQueen, *Toronto Daily Star*. ts, 2 pp.

12 June. Hon. Edmund Davie Fulton, Minister of Justice, Department of Justice, Ottawa. ts, 5 pp.

27 June. Rt. Rev. Angus MacQueen, London, Ont. ts, 3 pp., with 8 pp. ts draft copies attached.

29 June. The Editor, *San Francisco Chronicle*. ts, 1 p.

3 July. Rt. Rev. A.J. MacQueen, London, Ont. ts, 1 p.

6 July. The Editor, *Saturday Night*, Toronto. ts, 1 p.

22 July. The Editor, *Saturday Night*, Toronto. ts, 1 p.

15 August. J.K. [Jack Kent] Cooke, Publisher, *Saturday Night*, Toronto. ts, 1 p.

17 August. The Editor, *Toronto Daily Star*. ts, 1 p.

1960

8 February. The Editor, *Maclean's*, Toronto. ts, 1 p.

26 February. The Editor, *Hush Free Press*, Toronto. ts, 1 p.

26 February. Albert J. de Dion, Chairman, New York Area Council, The Mattachine Society, Inc., New York. ts, 2 pp.

17 March. Leslie F. Hannon, *Maclean's*, Toronto. ts, 1 p.

18 March. "Mailbag" Editor, *Maclean's*, Toronto. ts, 1 p.

26 March. Leslie F. Hannon, *Maclean's*, Toronto. ts, 1 p.

11 April. Pierre Berton, *Toronto Daily Star*. ts, 1 p.

11 April. Robert Fulford, *Toronto Daily Star*. ts, 1 p.

12 April. Nathan Cohen, *Toronto Daily Star*. ts, 1 p.

12 June. "Mailbag," *Maclean's*, Toronto. ts, 1 p.

28 June. *Toronto Daily Star*. ts, 1 p.

5 July. Pierre Berton, *Toronto Daily Star*. ts, 1 p.

5 July. Bureau of Accuracy, *Toronto Daily Star*. ts, 1 p.

5 July. "Mailbag," *Maclean's*, Toronto. ts, 1 p.

21 July. The Editor, *Saturday Night*, Toronto. ts, 1 p.

[undated, late September.] The Editor, *Globe and Mail*, Toronto. ts, 2 pp.

25 October. F.W. Robertson, *Globe and Mail*, Toronto. ts, 2 pp.

28 December. Frank Rasky, *Liberty*, Toronto. ts, 1 p.

1961

9 February. Dr. M.D. Touchtie, Forensic Clinic, Toronto. ts, 2 pp.

22 April. Pierre Berton, *Toronto Daily Star*. ts, 1 p.

12 May. Letters, *Newsweek*, New York. ts, 1 p.

1962

1 February. Letters, *Newsweek*, New York. ts, 1 p.

16 February. Department of Citizenship and Immigration, Ottawa. ts, 1 p.

26 February. The Editor, *Saturday Night*, Toronto. ts, 1 p.

30 March. Dwight W. Norris, *Newsweek*, New York. ts, 1 p.

28 December. Leonard Bertin, *Toronto Daily Star*. ts, 1 p.

1963

[undated, early March.] Pierre Berton, Contributing Editor, *Maclean's*, Toronto. ts, 3 pp. draft, with heavy annotations.

20 May. Ontario Human Rights Commission, Toronto. ts, 1 p.

23 May. E.A. Schofield, Civil Service Commission, Ottawa. ts, 1 p.

[undated, late May.] The Editor, *News-Observer*, Toronto. ts, 1 p., with annotations.

[undated, May-September.] The Editor, *Saturday Night*, Toronto. ts, 1 p.

[undated, 18-23 October.] Nathan Cohen, *Toronto Daily Star*. ts, 2 pp., with attached revised 4 pp. ts version of "Civil Liberties and the Homosexual."

14 November. The Editor, *Globe and Mail*, Toronto. ts, 1 p., with annotations, with 4 pp. of ts draft notes attached.

[undated, after 19 December.] The Editor, *Globe and Mail*, Toronto. ts, 2 pp.

1964

[undated, mid-January.] The Editor, *Toronto Daily Star*. ts, 1 p.

Correspondence Received by Jim Egan

1950

2 March. Brandt Aymar, Vice President, Greenberg Publishers, New York. ts, 1 p.

20 March. Nial Kent, [s.l.]. ts, 2 pp.

18 July. Carl W. Loveday, Assistant to the Publisher, Volitant Publishing Corporation, New York. ts, 1 p.

19 July. Tom Morgan, Editor, "Sound and Fury," *Esquire*, New York. ts, 1 p.

4 August. (Mrs.) Judith H. Drucker, Secretary to the Editor, *Parents' Magazine*, New York. ts, 1 p.

10 August. Hugh MacNair Kahler, Associate Editor, *Ladies' Home Journal*, Philadelphia. ts, 1 p.

21 August. [Unsigned], Associate Editor, *Coronet Magazine*, New York. ts form letter, 1 p.

21 August. Douglas E. Lurton, *Your Life*, The Kingsway Press, Inc., New York. ts, 1 p.

[undated, September?] The Editors, *Redbook Magazine*, New York. ts form letter, 1 p.

6 September. Hermann Mannheim, Editor, *British Journal of Delinquency*, London. ts, 1 p.

8 September. Helene Richards, Editorial Staff, *Coronet Magazine*, New York. ts, 1 p.

30 September. Signature illegible: J. O'B——, Secretary, Embassy of Ireland, Ottawa. ts, 1 p.

2 October. C.M. Sakellaropoulo, Ambassador of Greece, Royal Greek Embassy, Ottawa. ts, 1 p.

2 October. Signature illegible: Daniel F——, Royal Norwegian Legation, Ottawa. ts, 1 p.

2 October. Signature illegible: E. D————, Consular Officer, Turkish Embassy, Ottawa. ts, 1 p.

3 October. F.M. Forde, High Commissioner, Australian High Commissioner's Office, Ottawa. ts, 1 p.

3 October. Mariano de Yturralde, Consul General for Spain, Montreal. ts, 1 p.

3 October. H. Zoelly, Secretary of Legation, Legation of Switzerland in Canada, Ottawa. ts, 1 p. with 1 p. attached.

4 October. Baron P. de Gaiffier d'Hestroy, Counsellor of the Belgian Embassy, Ottawa. ts, 1 p. with 1 p. attached.

4 October. N.R. Perry, Official Secretary, Office of the High Commissioner for New Zealand, Ottawa. ts, 1 p.

5 October. A. Gordon Huson, Director, United Kingdom Information Office, Ottawa. ts, 1 p.

10 October. P.K. Banerjee, Second Secretary, Office of the High Commissioner for India, Ottawa. ts, 1 p.

10 October. Sigge de Lilliehook, Second Secretary, Legation of Sweden, Ottawa. ts, 1 p. with 1 p. attached.

11 October. H. Kessler, Attaché, Polish Legation, Ottawa. ts, 1 p.

11 October. Michel de Warenghien, Service d'Information Francais, Ottawa. ts, 1 p.

12 October. E.J. Garland, Minister of Canada to Norway, Canadian Legation, Oslo. ts, 1 p.

13 October. F.M. Forde, High Commissioner, Australian High Commissioner's Office, Ottawa. ts, 1 p.

16 October. Olavi Lahonen, Secretary of Legation, Legation of Finland, Ottawa. ts, 1 p.

16 October. A.W. Steward, Information Officer, Office of the High Commissioner, Union of South Africa, Ottawa. ts, 1 p.

16 October. A.D. Vas Nunes, Secretary of Embassy, Netherlands Embassy, Ottawa. ts, 1 p.

19 October. Signature illegible: William Duff ?, Ministry of Home Affairs,

Stormont, Belfast, Northern Ireland. ts, 1 p. with 1 p. attached.

27 October. [To Leo Engle.] William L. Fendley, Batavia, N.Y. ts, 1 p.

27 October. [To Leo Engle.] Z. [Zigurds] Vitols, Winnipeg. ms, 3 pp.

28 October. Luis Fernandez MacGregor, Counsellor of the Embassy of Mexico, Ottawa. ts, 1 p.

[undated, November?] [To Leo Engle.] Marvin J. Budderman, Fairmont, Minn. ms, 2 pp.

[undated, November?] [To Leo Engle.] H. Koala, Ingersoll, Ont. ts, 2 pp.

[undated, November?] [To Leo Engle.] Carl Peer, Beloit, Wis. ms, 1 p.

6 November. Signature illegible: Don Bell ?, Toronto. ms, 2 pp.

8 November. Francesca L. Welch, Editor, *Sir!*, Volitant Publishing Corporation, New York. ts, 1 p.

14 November. Belgian Embassy, Ottawa. ts, 1 p. with 1 p. attached.

17 November. J.C.G. Brown, for the Minister, Canadian Legation, Berne, Switzerland. ts, 1 p. with 5 pp. attached.

17 November. [To Leo Engle.] Charles H.W. Maynard, Arrow Lakes, Needles, B.C. ts, 1 p.

22 November. [To Leo Engle.] Vannoy Lane Stokes, Bay St. Louis, Miss. ts, 1 p.

22 November. A.W. Steward, Information Officer, Office of the High Commissioner, Union of South Africa, Ottawa. ts, 1 p.

24 November. Maxwell Dean, Associated Editor, Exposition Press, New York. ts, 1 p.

28 November. N.R. Perry, Official Secretary, Office of the High Commissioner for New Zealand, Ottawa. ts, 1 p.

1 December. Olavi Lahonen, Secretary of Legation, Legation of Finland, Ottawa. ts, 2 pp. with 1 p. attached.

12 December. Signature illegible: A.Y., *Sexology Magazine*, New York. ts, 1 p.

28 December. Dr. Louis Franklin Freed, Johannesburg. ts, 2 pp.

1951

10 January. [Unsigned], Editorial Department, *Sexology Magazine*, New York. ts, 1 p.

16 January. Henry Gerber, Washington, D.C. ts, 1 p., with photograph attached.

24 January. K. East, Office of the High Commissioner for the United Kingdom, Ottawa. ts, 1 p. with 3 pp. attached.

27 January. Henry [Gerber], Washington, D.C. ts, 2 pp.

29 January. Dr. Aujaleu, For the Minister, The Director of Social Hygiene, Social Hygiene Management, Ministry of Public Health and of Population, Paris, France. ts, 2 pp. with 2 pp. translation attached.

1 February. (Miss) Betty Bunn, *Sir!*, Volitant Publishing Corporation, New York. ts, 1 p.

5 February. Dr. Louis Franklin Freed, Johannesburg. ms, 1 p.

7 February. Henry [Gerber], Washington, D.C. ts, 4 pp.

25 February. Henry [Gerber], Washington, D.C. ts, 2 pp.

26 February. Dr. D.O. Cauldwell, *Sexology Magazine*, New York. ts, 2 pp.

5 March. Henry [Gerber], Washington, D.C. ts, 4 pp.

12 March. Dr. D.O. Cauldwell, Vida, Ala. ts, 4 pp.

15 March. William C. Lengel, Editor-in-Chief, Gold Medal Books, Fawcett Publications, Inc., New York. form letter ts, 1 p.

28 March. Henry [Gerber], Washington, D.C. ts, 4 pp.

5 April. Dr. D.O. Cauldwell, Vida, Ala. ts, 1 p.

10 April. Henry [Gerber], Washington, D.C. ts, 2 pp.

13 April. Henry Gerber, Washington, D.C. ts, 1 p.

16 April. Henry Gerber, Washington, D.C. ts, 2 pp.

17 April. Barbara Grigg, for the Editors, *Time Magazine*, New York. ts, 1 p.

23 April. Dr. D.O. Cauldwell, Vida, Ala. ts, 2 pp.

23 April. Henry [Gerber], Washington, D.C. ts, 1 p.

25 April. D.S. for August Lenniger, August Lenniger Literary Agency, New York. ts, 1 p.

7 May. Nicolas A. Anissas, Ambassador of Greece, Royal Greek Embassy, Ottawa. ts, 1 p.

9 May. Henry [Gerber], Passau, Bavaria. ts, 2 pp.

25 October. Miss K. Rukmini, Second Secretary, Office of the High Commissioner for India, Ottawa. ts, 1 p. with 1 p. attached.

1952

25 January. Ruth Jones, Editor, "The Writer's Market," *Writer's Digest*, Cincinnati. ts, 1 p.

5 February. Dorothy Babineau, for Information Officer, Union of South Africa Government Information Office, Ottawa. ts, 1 p.

28 February. Jerry Tax, *U.S. Crime Magazine*, New York. ts, 1 p.

30 April. Jeremiah Tax, *U.S. Crime Magazine*, New York. ts, 1 p.

29 August. Burt Carver, Associate Editor, Exposition Press, Inc., New York. ts, 1 p.

9 September. Burt Carver, Associate Editor, Exposition Press, Inc., New York. ts, 1 p.

7 October. Annette Van Howe, Associate Editor, *Brief Magazine*, New York. ts, 1 p.

1953

26 February. Alfred F. Islan, Jr., Managing Editor, *Saga — The Magazine of True Adventure*, New York. ts, 1 p.

11 March. Maxwell Hamilton, *Blue Book Magazine*, New York. ts, 1 p.

23 March. Joseph Corona, Editor, *Adam — A Man's Magazine*, Fawcett Publications, Inc., New York. ts, 1 p.

8 April. Joseph Corona, Editor, *Adam — A Man's Magazine*, Fawcett Publications, Inc., New York. ts, 1 p.

28 April. Lawrence Sanders, Editor, *Man's Magazine*, New York. ts, 1 p.

29 June. Theodore Irwin, Editor, *Real Magazine*, New York. ts, 1 p.

20 August. Ken Burns, Chairman, The Mattachine Society, Los Angeles. ts, 1 p.

7 September. Theodore Irwin, Editor, *Real Magazine*, New York. ms, 1 p.

23 December. Philip H. Daniels, *Justice Weekly*, Toronto. ts, 1 p.

1954

7 January. William Lambert [pseud. of W. Dorr Legg], Business Manager, ONE, Incorporated, Los Angeles. ts, 1 p.

15 March. Don F. Brown, M.P., House of Commons, Ottawa. ts, 1 p.

19 March. A. Small, Clerk of the Joint Committee on Capital and Corporal Punishment and Lotteries, House of Commons, Ottawa. ts, 1 p.

19 March. Keith Vogel, Private Secretary, Minister of Justice and Attorney General of Canada, Ottawa. ts, 1 p.

20 October. R. Woody Gregory, Editorial Secretary, ONE, Incorporated, Los Angeles. ts, 1 p.

15 November. R. Woody Gregory, Editorial Secretary, ONE, Incorporated, Los Angeles. ts, 1 p.

23 November. Vyvyan Holland, London. ms, 1 p.

1958

1 February. R.L. Chiocchetti, Westree, Ont. ts, 1 p.

28 June. Albert J. de Dion, Vice-Chairman, New York Area Council, The Mattachine Society, Inc., New York. form letter ts, 1 p.

1 October. Calvin Hoffman, Belle Harbor, N.Y. ts, 1 p.

1959

[undated, early 1959?] Shelton Dewey, Glendale, Ca. ts, 1 p., with 2 ts. pp. attached.

3 February. Robert D. Van Horn, Columbus, Ohio. ts, 1 p.

16 February. G.L. Bennett, Director of Port Administration, Customs and Excise, Department of National Revenue, Ottawa. ts, 1 p.

21 March. Shelton Dewey, Glendale, Ca. ts, 1 p.

4 May. Jim Kepner, Los Angeles. ts, 1 p.

29 May. D.H.W. Henry, Acting Director, Criminal Law Section, Department of Justice, Ottawa. ts, 1 p.

1 June. James H. Felmey, Bridgeton, N.J. ms, 5 pp.

21 June. Angus J. MacQueen, Moderator, The General Council, The United Church of Canada, London, Ont. ms, 3 pp.

1 July. A.J. MacQueen, Moderator, Office of the General Council, The United Church of Canada, Toronto. ms, 2 pp.

23 July. W.R. Jacket, Deputy Minister of Justice, Department of Justice, Ottawa. ts, 1 p.

8 August. Robert Fulford, *Toronto Daily Star*. ts, 2 pp.

18 August. Arnold Edinborough, Editor, *Saturday Night*, Toronto. ts, 1 p.

29 August. Shelton Dewey, Glendale, Ca. ts, 1 p.

10 November. A.J. MacQueen, First-St. Andrew's United Church of Canada, London, Ont. ms, 1 p.

7 December. Jim [Kepner], ONE, Incorporated, Los Angeles. ts, 1 p.

9 December. Sarah Winter, *Time Magazine*, New York. ts, 1 p.

29 December. J.V. Kingsbury, Executive Editor, Toronto Star Limited. ts, 1 p.

1960

[undated, January.] Daniel Cappiello, Brookline, Mass. ms, 2 pp.

3 January. Mrs. Venetia Newall, Joint-Secretary, The Homosexual Law Reform Society, London. ts, 1 p.

21 January. Nathan Cohen, Entertainment Editor, Toronto Star Limited. ts, 1 p.

4 February. Dan Cappiello, Brookline, Mass. ms, 2 pp.

5 February. Nathan Cohen, Toronto Star Limited. ts, 1 p.

15 February. Rev. A. Hallidie Smith, Secretary, The Homosexual Law Reform Society, London. ts, 1 p., with annotations.

16 February. Leslie F. Hannon, Managing Editor, *Maclean's*, Toronto. ts, 1 p.

16 February. Donald S. Lucas, Secretary-General, The Daily Committee, The Mattachine Society, Inc., San Francisco. form letter ts, 1 p. With attachment dated 12 February 1960 from the San Francisco Area Council, The Mattachine Society ("Open Letter to Members of the Mattachine Society"). form letter and reports, ts, 7 pp.

[undated, late February.] Illegible signature: Howard ——, [San Francisco]. ts note, 1 p., with attachments.

8 March. Jim [Kepner], ONE, Incorporated, Los Angeles. ts, 1 p.

10 March. Albert J. de Dion, Chairman, New York Area Council, The Mattachine Society, Inc., New York. ts, 1 p.

10 March. Margaret E. Fleming, Statistician, Analysis Section, Census Division, Dominion Bureau of Statistics, Ottawa. ts, 1 p., with tables attached.

24 March. Sally Hurst, Secretary to Leslie F. Hannon, *Maclean's*, Toronto. ts, 1 p.

24 March. Reg. M. Suthern, Wolfville, N.S. ms, 1 p.

24 March. Joan Weatherseed, for the Editors, *Maclean's*, Toronto. ts, 1 p.

27 March. Bill Hatter, Niagara Falls, Ont. ms, 1 p.

30 March. Don Roberts, New York. ts, 2 pp.

31 March. W.R. (Bill) Brown, Sudbury, Ont. ms, 1 p.

4 April. Donald S. Lucas, Secretary-General, The Daily Committee, The Mattachine Society, Inc., San Francisco. form letter ts, 1 p. With attachment dated 13 March 1960 ("Open Letter to All Mattachine Members") from Albert J. de Dion, Chairman, New York Area Council, The Mattachine Society, Inc., New York. form letter ts, 2 pp.

5 April. Albert J. de Dion, Chairman, New York Area Council, The Mattachine Society, Inc., New York. ts, 1 p. With attachment dated 13 March 1960 ("Open Letter to All Mattachine Members") from Albert J. de Dion, Chairman, New York Area Council, The Mattachine Society, Inc., New York. form letter ts, 2 pp.

7 April. James N. Johnson, Glencoe, Ont. ms, 2 pp.

14 April. Robert Fulford, Toronto Star Limited. ts, 1 p.

16 May. Signature illegible: pp Walter van Woensel, Secretary, International Committee for Sexual Equality (I.C.S.E.), Amsterdam. ts, 1 p.

24 May. Joyce Davidson, Canadian Broadcasting Corporation, Toronto. ts, 1 p.

25 May. A.W. Nicol, Executive Officer, Office of the Attorney General, Ontario, Toronto. ts, 1 p.

June. Ronald Payne, Circulation Manager, *New Statesman*, London. form letter ts, 1 p.

5 July. T.J.G. Williams, Toronto. ts, 1 p.

6 July. J.V. Kingsbury, Executive Editor, Toronto Star Limited. ts, 1 p.

10 July. T.J.G. Williams, Toronto. ts, 3 pp.

12 July. Pierre Berton, Associate Editor, Toronto Star Limited. ts, 1 p.

25 July. Pierre Berton, Associate Editor, Toronto Star Limited. ts, 1 p.

18 October. F.W. Robertson, Associate Editor, *Globe and Mail*, Toronto. ts, 1 p.

11 November. Sidney Katz, Associate Editor, *Maclean's*, Toronto. ts, 1 p.

30 November. Nathan Cohen, Toronto Star Limited. ts, 1 p.

23 December. Venetia Newall, The Homosexual Reform Society, London. Receipt and separate compliments slip.

1961

[undated, 1961?] Antony Grey, Secretary, Albany Trust, London. ts, 1 p., with attached receipt.

13 February [1961?] Venetia Newall, The Homosexual Reform Society, London. ms, 1 p.

20 April. Donald S. Lucas, Secretary-General, The Mattachine Society, Inc., San Francisco. ts, 1 p.

31 May. Dwight W. Norris, for the Editors, *Newsweek*, New York. ts, 1 p.

12 July. Mrs. Venetia Newall, Trustee and Secretary, The Albany Trust, London. ts, 1 p.

18 August. Ron Haggart, Toronto Star Limited. ts, 1 p.

[undated, late 1961?] Venetia Newall, The Homosexual Law Reform Society, London. ms, 2 pp.

1962

11 January. Patrick Watson, Producer, "Inquiry," Canadian Broadcasting Corporation, Toronto. ts, 1 p.

18 January. Patrick Watson, Producer, "Inquiry," Canadian Broadcasting Corporation, Toronto. ts, 1 p.

10 February. Albert J. de Dion, Chairman, The Mattachine Society, Inc., of New York. ts, 1 p.

26 February. E.P. Beasley, Chief, Admissions Division, Immigration Branch, Department of Citizenship and Immigration, Ottawa. ts, 1 p.

12 March. Angus J. MacQueen, First-St. Andrew's United Church of Canada, London, Ont. ms, 1 p.

21 March. Dwight W. Norris, for the Editors, *Newsweek*, New York. ts, 1 p. [The original of this letter does not survive in Egan's papers, but there is a copy that was re-typed by Egan.]

[undated, April?] F. v. Mechelin, President, International Committee for Sexual Equality (I.C.S.E.), Amsterdam. ts form letter, 2 pp. [2 copies.]

1963

24 January. J. Foome, International Committee for Sexual Equality (I.C.S.E.), Amsterdam. ts, 1 p.

11 February. Norman Jones, Scarborough, Ont. ts, 3 pp.

15 March. Pierre Berton, Contributing Editor, *Maclean's*, Toronto. ts, 1 p.

28 March. Bill [W. Dorr Legg?], ONE, Incorporated, Los Angeles. ts note, 1 p.

6 April. Bill [W. Dorr Legg?], ONE, Incorporated, Los Angeles. ts note, 1 p. with three pp. ts attached.

17 May. E.A. Schofield, Assistant Secretary, Civil Service Commission, Ottawa. ts, 1 p.

29 May. Eric A. Schofield, Assistant Secretary, Civil Service Commission, Ottawa. ts, 2 pp.

30 May. Daniel G. Hill, Director, Ontario Human Rights Commission, Toronto. ts, 1 p.

7 June. Tom Waugh, [Toronto]. ms, 1 p.

12 August. Joan Fraser, Chairman, ECHO Convention Committee, The Mattachine Society, Inc., of New York. form letter ts, 1 p.

22 August. Albert J. de Dion, ECHO Delegate [and Chairman, The Mattachine Society, Inc., of New York]. form letter ts, 1 p.

24 September. Pierre Berton, "The Pierre Berton Hour," Toronto. ts, 1 p.

25 September. Joan Wharton, for the Editors, *Newsweek*, New York. ts, 1 p.

18 October. Nathan Cohen, Editor, Entertainment and Special Features, Toronto Star Limited. ts, 2 pp.

27 December. Pierre Berton, "The Pierre Berton Show," Toronto. ts, 1 p.

1964

13 February. Tom Allen, Associate Editorial Page Editor, Toronto Star Limited. ts, 1 p.

14 February. Sid Katz, *Maclean's*, Toronto. ts, 1 p.

22 April. Don Obe, Page Seven Editor, *Toronto Telegram*. ts, 1 p.

26 May. John Aitken, Page Seven Editor, *Toronto Telegram*. ts, 1 p.

Restricted Correspondence

There is one folder of restricted correspondence in the Egan papers. It contains mostly personal letters from individuals. Egan conducted a steady and voluminous correspondence with some of these individuals, but no copies of his letters to them survive in his papers. Please note that the letters in this folder may not be examined or quoted without the permission of Mr. Egan. The letters include:

Father Bernard, Saint George Chapel and Monastery, The Church of Divine Love — Orthodox, Las Vegas, Nev. ts, 1 p., dated 4 March 1959.

Marv Budderman, Fairmont, Minn., and Chicago. Nine letters from Fairmont, Minn., six are ts, three are ms, total 18 pp. All are undated except for three, which are dated January-February 1951. Seven ms. letters from Chicago, total 24 pp. All are undated except for one, which is dated 3 June 1951. In addition, there are two undated black and white photographs of Budderman.

Roland Chiocchetti, Sudbury, Ont. Four ts letters, 1 p. each, dated 18 February, 26 February, 25 May, and 1 July 1959.

Bill Hatter, Niagara Falls, Ont. Three ms letters, 3 pp., 2 pp., and 2 pp., dated 31 March, 6 April, and 18 April 1960.

Bob Jennings, Philadelphia. ts, 2 pp., dated 10 January 1960.

Charles H.W. Maynard, Needles, B.C., and Edgewood, B.C. Ten letters (eight ms, two ts), total 19 pp. All are dated between 18 November 1950 and 16 May 1951. The first letter is addressed to Adrian B. Lopez, Editor of *Sir!*, and was passed on to "Leo Engle." In addition, there is one undated photograph of Maynard.

Allan Miller, Toronto. Two ts letters, 2 pp. and 5 pp., undated [ca. 1960].

Carl Peer, Beloit, Wis. ms, 1 p., undated [ca. 1951].

Don Roberts, New York. ts, 2 pp., dated 19 April 1960, with 1 p. ts note attached from William Lambert (pseud. of W. Dorr Legg), ONE, Incorporated, to Don Roberts dated 1 April 1960.

Reg Suthern, Wolfville, N.S. ts, 1 p., dated 29 March 1960.

T——, [n.p.] ts, 1 p., dated 10 September ——.

Ziggy [Zigurds Vitols], Winnipeg. ms, 2 pp., dated 14 November 1950.

Index

A Note on the Author and the Compiler

Jim Egan lives in Courtenay, B.C., with Jack Nesbit, his partner of fifty years.

Don McLeod is the author or compiler of five books, including *Lesbian and Gay Liberation in Canada: A Selected Annotated Chronology, 1964-1975* (ECW Press/Homewood Books, 1996). He is a longtime volunteer at the Canadian Lesbian and Gay Archives in Toronto.